ARNULF RAINER

THIS EXHIBITION IS SUPPORTED BY:

AUSTRIAN FEDERAL MINISTRY OF CULTURAL AFFAIRS

OFFICE OF CULTURAL AFFAIRS OF THE CITY OF VIENNA

AUSTRIAN FEDERAL ECONOMIC CHAMBER

AUSTRIAN NATIONAL TOURIST OFFICE

AUSTRIAN AIRLINES

ⓒ **CREDITANSTALT**

OESTERREICHISCHE LAENDERBANK ▬

ZUMTOBEL ///   *LIGHTING THE WAY*

ARNULF RAINER

An exhibition curated by
R. H. Fuchs

Solomon R. Guggenheim Museum, New York

This book is published in conjunction with the exhibition *Arnulf Rainer* at the Solomon R. Guggenheim Museum, New York (May 13-July 9, 1989); Museum of Contemporary Art, Chicago (July 29-October 15, 1989); Historisches Museum der Stadt Wien, Vienna (November-December 1989); Haags Gemeentemuseum, The Hague (January-February 1990).

The exhibition is organized by the Haags Gemeentemuseum, The Hague, in collaboration with the Solomon R. Guggenheim Museum, New York.

The essay by R. H. Fuchs and the essays by Arnulf Rainer were translated by Beate Gibbon, Bielefeld, except the essay *Lamentation*. The essay by Franz Dahlem was translated by John William Gabriel, Worpswede. All texts were edited by Carol Fuerstein and Diana Murphy.

Front Cover: Arnulf Rainer *Untitled*, 1974, Collection Solomon R. Guggenheim Museum, New York. Gift, Montedison, U.S.A., 1986

Published by
ARGE Gabriele Wimmer & John Sailer
21 Opernring
A-1010 Vienna
Austria

Soft cover edition not available to the trade

Layout by Franz Harreither, Zell am See
Typesetting by Lasersatz Josef Maringer, Maishofen
Color separations by Repro Brüll, Saalfelden
Printed and bound by Welsermühl, Druck- und Verlagshaus AG, Wels

Printed in Austria

ISBN 3-85127-005-3

Contents

Lenders to the Exhibition

Austria Tabak, Vienna

Galerie Heike Curtze, Vienna/Dusseldorf

Komm.-Rat. Karlheinz Essl, Klosterneuburg, Austria

Hessisches Landesmuseum, Darmstadt

Mr. and Mrs. William Hokin, Chicago

Sabine Knust, Maximilianverlag, Munich

Karlheinz Kossdorff, Vienna

E. and H. Kranz, Dusseldorf

Collection Mr. and Mrs. Ronald S. Lauder, New York

Galerie Lelong, Zürich

m Bochum, Galerie für Film, Foto, Neue Konkrete Kunst und Video, Bochum

The Museum of Modern Art, New York

Arnulf Rainer, Vienna

Dr. Dr. h. c. Gerhard Schomburg, Mülheim/Ruhr

The Prince of Schwarzenberg, Vienna

Solomon R. Guggenheim Museum, New York

Dr. Reiner Speck, Cologne

Dr. Heliod Spiekermann, Haan

Städtische Galerie im Lenbachhaus, Munich

Stedelijk Van Abbemuseum, Eindhoven

Galerie Ulysses, Vienna

Prof. Dr. Felix Unger, Salzburg

Dr. Helmut Zambo, Dusseldorf/Vienna

Private Collections in Austria, Federal Republic of Germany, France and Switzerland

Acknowledgments

This is the first museum exhibition of Arnulf Rainer's work in the United States. I am most pleased to be able to present the oeuvre of this major European painter to a New York audience as part of the Guggenheim Museum's ongoing program of a exhibitions devoted to contemporary international art. I wish to extend thanks to the many individuals who have helped to realize the show, which will travel in the United States and Europe after its premiere in New York.

First and foremost, I am indebted to Rudi Fuchs, Director of the Haags Gemeentemuseum and the Castello di Rivoli, Turin, who made the thoughtful selection of Rainer's works spanning the artist's career from the 1950s to the present and thus providing a broad overview of his oeuvre. Mr. Fuchs's insightful essay is an important part of the catalogue. I would like to acknowledge the efforts of my colleague Diane Waldman, Deputy Director of the Guggenheim Museum, who wrote the informative foreword to this publication and, acting as project director, contributed significantly to the success of the presentation in New York.

This exhibition could not have been realized without the extensive funding provided by numerous sponsors. Dr. Franz Vranitzky, Federal Chancellor of the Republic of Austria, was instrumental at a critical time in arranging financial support from several departments of the Austrian government. The assistance of Dr. Eva Nowotny, Foreign Policy Advisor, and Dr. Paul Andreas Mailath-Pokorny, Public Relations Manager, is gratefully acknowledged as well. I express thanks to Dr. Hilde Hawlicek, Federal Minister of Cultural Affairs, for the generous contribution made by her department, and to Josef Secky of the Ministry of Cultural Affairs. Further, I wish to acknowledge Dr. Ursula Pasterk, Commissioner of Cultural Affairs of the City of Vienna, whose gracious efforts helped to secure financial support from her administration. Deep appreciation is also extended to the following individuals and organizations for their funding of the exhibition: Rudolf Sallinger, President of the Austrian Economic Chamber; Dr. Klaus Lukas, Director of the Austrian National Tourist Office; Dr. Anton Heschgl and Dr. Hubert Papousek, Presidents of Austrian Airlines, the official overseas carrier for this exhibition; Dr. Herbert Bammer, Sales Manager of Austrian Airlines; Dr. Guido N. Schmidt-Chiari, Chairman of the Managing Board, Nikolaus Dreihann-Holenia, Senior Manager and Deputy Head, and Dr. Diemuth Kastner, Senior Manager, all of Creditanstalt; Dkfm. Gerhard Wagner, Chairman of the Board of Managing Directors, and Dr. Karl Mauk, both of Oesterreichische Laenderbank; and Dipl.-Ing. Jürg Zumtobel, Manager of the Board of Zumtobel AG.

Many difficult logistical problems have been gracefully resolved with the aid of John Sailer and Gabriele Wimmer, Directors of the Galerie Ulysses in Vienna. Their assistance in the organization of this exhibition is greatly appreciated, as is the aid of Agnes Kammerlander, also of Galerie Ulysses. Without these individuals, the exhibition might not have reached fruition. Peter Marboe's assistance during early discussions about this exhibition also must be mentioned.

The staff of the Guggenheim Museum deserves praise for overseeing the many details that such a project necessarily entails. Among the individuals who have devoted their time and efforts here, I wish to thank Susan Hapgood and Susan B. Hirschfeld, who coordinated the New York presentation; Carol Fuerstein and Diana Murphy, who edited the catalogue; Victoria Hertz, who assisted with the transportation arrangements for the works; and Clare Bell and Patricia de Alvear.

To all of the lenders, I extend my gratitude for agreeing to part with their works for the duration of the show. Finally, on behalf of everyone associated with the project, I wish to express indebtedness to the artist himself whose creative contributions constitute this presentation.

Thomas Krens
Director
The Solomon R. Guggenheim Foundation

Acknowledgments

The Arnulf Rainer exhibition was proposed to Thomas M. Messer and Diane Waldman. One hopes such an exhibition leads to a better understanding of Rainer's unique painting. That would be good for everybody in art. I thank my former colleague for accepting the idea and I thank my present colleague, Thomas Krens, for his courage to continue the Guggenheim's involvement with European art. To Diane Waldman and her staff I am grateful, especially to Susan Hapgood and to Carol Fuerstein who edited my text. I am very pleased that Bruce Guenther consented to have the exhibition in Chicago.

The exhibition would not have succeeded without the cheerful help of Gabriele Wimmer, who manages Rainer's office, and of John Sailer, who coordinated the production of the catalogue. To all lenders I am deeply greateful. Arnulf Rainer followed the proceedings with his usual mixture of enthusiasm and mild scepticism. The painting is his — but for any errors in the exhibition I am responsible.

Rudi Fuchs
Director
Gemeentemuseum, The Hague

Foreword

Like many other European artists, Arnulf Rainer is viewed as a major figure abroad but is little known to audiences in the United States. The Joseph Beuys exhibition, held at the Guggenheim Museum in 1980, was a milestone in terms of awakening Americans to such an artist. It presented a body of work known only to a few in this country, opened the door to questions about American awareness of European art and led to a reevaluation of the concept of the hegemony of the United States in the international art-world. This stunning exhibition was followed by a series of equally revelatory presentations in Europe of the work of a younger generation of painters who burst on the scene in Germany and Italy in the early 1980s. The recognition accorded these Neo-Expressionists, whose painting represented a radical departure from Minimalism and Conceptualism, which were largely American in origin and were the predominant movements from the mid-1960s through the 1970s, led to a renewed interest in their postwar precursors. Many other artists who, like Beuys, belonged to the generation of the 1950s and early 1960s were looked at with new insight and brought to the attention of Americans. It is in the context of this reexamination that the Rainer exhibition is presented at the Guggenheim Museum. American and European art evolved along parallel paths during the 1950s, for the most part sharing a basis in abstraction, but began to diverge in the 1960s with the development of Pop Art, Color Field painting and Minimalism in the United States. Although these movements found their adherents in Europe, they did not take hold to the same degree as in the States. Instead Europe saw the emergence of unique figures like Beuys and Francis Bacon, who were not clearly identified with larger movements or groups. This singularity obtains also with Rainer who carries on many of the traditions of prewar Dada and Expressionism while bringing a new sense of urgency to these pioneering movements.

Born on December 8, 1929, in Baden, a small town twenty miles south of Vienna, Rainer was largely self-taught as an artist and began at an early age to draw from nature. By 1948 he had discovered Surrealism, the most important and influential style of the 1920s and 1930s, and was attracted to the movement's theoretical positions, in particular its emphasis on automatism which liberated the imagination and allowed the artist to give concrete form to the emotions, dreams and desires that ensued. Rainer began to practice automatism based on the model of Surrealism, producing imagery disposed in allover compositions. By 1951, however, he had rejected this imagery in favor of nearly abstract, virtually monochromatic black drawings which issued from automatic techniques.

Between 1951 and 1952 Rainer refined and elaborated his concept of automatism in such works as his *Microstructures, Optical Decentralizations, Blind Drawings* and *Centralizations.* However, he is best known for his *Overpaintings,* serial works begun in 1953 in which he effaces his own images and the paintings of other artists. In concert with the development of the *Overpaintings,* he started to work with photographs of his own body and to examine the nature of color relationships and the possibilities of the shaped canvas. His involvement with Surrealist automatism led him to pursue Action Painting, which became his primary means of expression during the 1950s: he worked quickly, intuitively and spontaneously.

In 1964, while living in Berlin, the artist began to experiment with hallucinogenic drugs, the use of which led him to a greater awareness of aspects of the nervous system and the musculature of the body, a development with important ramifications for his work. Rainer speaks of the use of his own image as an attempt to expand the "visual formulation of the possible, the imagined." He adds:

> *I grab my hair and pull. I jump without reason, mimic discoveries, draw visions, lie and lie, until it could become true. I make no attempt at a one to one correspondence. I let it happen through an act of reproduction.*
>
> *My own ideas, corrections, idealizations, develop in three phases: first scenic, extracted photographically. It must be reduced as much as possible, since it is concentrated in the instant that the camera records. Corrections aren't possible, only the instant counts. Most often I use a mirror, not as a control, but as a stimulation, to achieve a kind of extroverted communication with myself. Well defined, well motivated performances, known typecastings — as practised by actors — don't interest me. It is only in the realising that I can find, that I can look for, whatever it is that wants to activate itself within me.[1]*

Rainer's mature working method is similar to that of Dadaists such as Hans Arp. Like Arp in his chance collages, Rainer initially depends on accident and intuition and subsequently refines and redefines his images without, however, sacrificing the immediacy and spontaneity of his original impulse.

Rainer is drawn to primitive forms of art and seeks to communicate some of its basic expressiveness, which has been lost to our culture, through his own images. In this, he shares with many twentieth-century artists a desire to capture the force of a primary impulse. Interwoven with this positive quest is a profound sense of the absurd, a nihilism born of the European condition engendered by two World Wars and reinforced by the artist's image of himself as an isolated and alienated individual. Rainer can be compared to Yves Klein (1928-62), with whom he shares many attitudes. Klein possessed a restless and innovative imagination. An expert in judo and practitioner of Rosicrucianism, a believer in alchemy and levitation, he began to experiment with monochromy in the late 1940s. Klein developed a series of ultramarine blue canvases that expressed his concept of nothingness, experimented with the effects of rain and fire on pigment and produced *Anthropometrics* by covering nude models with blue paint and rolling them on bare canvases to create imprints of their forms. In his development and use of body-shadow prints and monochromatic paintings, Klein found the ultimate "representation of the immaterial, the sovereign liberation of the spirit."[2]

Both Rainer and Klein use the human body to express the inner being and their consciousness of themselves as artists. Rainer's anguish, his identification of the artist as an outcast, isolated from society, distinguishes him from the more extroverted Klein, however. Rainer and Klein share a belief in the efficacy of altered states and in the capacity of the human mind and imagination to transcend the human condition. Their own ability to enact this transcendence is made possible through hallucination, through a belief in magic and alchemy and through an acceptance of the supernatural as a precondition for existence in the natural world. Unlike Klein, whose subject in the monochrome canvases is the disembodied spirit, Rainer expresses the anguish of the corporeal in his *Overpaintings*; he needs a physical image, the self, as a jumping-off point for the netherworld of fire and brimstone, in which redemption is achieved through suffering and destruction is followed by regeneration. The two artists converge in their commitment to many central concepts of Dada and Surrealism and in their belief that art can be a cathartic force in society. They differ in their individual responses, which stem, in part, from their separate heritages: from Klein's uniquely French sense of irony and understatement and from Rainer's peculiarly Northern European anguish and expressionism. For Rainer, the exterior, the self, provides the passage to the interior world. And for him it is the interior world that represents true reality.

Diane Waldman
Deputy Director

1 Quoted in Muriel Emanuel et al., eds., *Contemporary Artists*, New York, 1983, pp. 766—777.
2 Quoted in H. H. Arnason, *History of Modern Art*, revised and enlarged edition, New York, 1985, p. 647.

Alceste, admirez la nuance
de ce jaune clair qui s'avance
sous cet incarnat velouté.

(Jules Pilet de la Mesnardière)

The Labyrinth

Rudi Fuchs

It is very much an art of the studio, the painting of Arnulf Rainer; the art of a painter locking himself in, almost hiding; of painting in solitude, absorbed by the studio, in contemplation, poised. He has written about those moments of waiting and despair and of the flight of fancy ending in disaster. He has written of the failure to get the image right, the right tension and the right temperature. At times the language is slightly rhetorical, like the speech of an actor, but there is no coyness. Life in the studio is not altogether pleasant, it seems. Maybe for that reason he has many studios, four or five at least, in Vienna and in the country; when remaining in one studio becomes too oppressive and difficult, he can move to the next and start again. But it is surprising, given the importance to him of working in the studio, that there are only a few photographs published of him at work. He is secretive. He hides his ways of painting just as the paintings hide and sometimes completely cover other images. The paintings show that painting them is an active and physical process, nervous and full of frenzy yet at times also carried out in a state of mystical resignation; but in the end the active process subsides, leaving the painting as it is, alone, abandoned. He has said that he goes on painting until he no longer sees any progress. Occasionally, when the session has been particularly wild when he has been doing fingerpaintings, for instance, smearing and slashing at twenty images simultaneously, he has to stop from sheer exhaustion. That does not mean, however, that paintings are then completed and finished. In the fresh light of another day some may look good, others miserable. But the judgment may change again the next day. He has become very good, Rainer, at waiting — at waiting for the day when he has enough distance to work on the paintings again. He has to wait until the memory of the previous session with a particular group of paintings has faded away; otherwise his memory might lead him back to the point where he previously had to abandon them. That would surely be the wrong place to start. But when he starts again, sometimes after years, it is not to make small changes or detailed improvements. He goes over the whole surface again; the painting may change completely. Life in the studio is a life, therefore, of going around in circles. He circles around his paintings, caged in the studio, like an animal of prey. But the movements shift and there is a certain progress. The progress is not the development of style or principle. In the mid-fifties, he

15

adopted the principle of *Übermalung* (overpainting) as a method. In later years that method remained the real basis for his work — but the work expanded when he found new motifs and thus the method also became more diversified. Since the time he started the *Übermalungen* he has usually painted on (or over or on top of) other images. The only notable exceptions are the hectic finger paintings from the mid-seventies onward. He works on other images, fencing with them, because they liberate and activate his creative energies. In front of a blank canvas he feels paralyzed, he has said. It is like the writer's fear of the white, empty sheet of paper. It is important to have another image in front of him — to attack, to improve, to deform, to vary, to accentuate, to emphasize, to cover up or to wipe out. Occasionally he has worked directly with other artists, namely with Dieter Rot or with Günter Brus; he worked with children and once he had a drawing session with a chimpanzee. But most of the time he uses photographs. Some isolated, earlier examples apart, this work with photographs began in earnest in the late sixties — with enlarged snapshots of his own contorted face, made in photo-booth in the railway station. Soon he began to use professional photographers to make these photographs of facial expressions, contortions and grimaces, and of all kinds of body poses into which he could twist himself. These images, wide-ranging in their kind of expressions became part of the studio. He was mainly working on *Crosses* and *Übermalungen* then, paintings and drawings, working slowly and evenly and tenaciously on the same surface, over and over. The curious, mobile photographs, showing movement arrested by the camera, suggested swifter, more impulsive, and also sketchier and more fragmentary kinds of expressive formulation. They expanded his vocabulary and intensified his instinct. Soon thereafter he began also to work on other material — photographs of female acrobats, lesbians, women in trances or in sexual ecstasy, "artistic" animals like peacocks and monkeys, death masks, the actor Bernhard Minetti, subterranean architecture, rock formations, faces of dead people, the portrait of Robespierre, images from nineteenth-century books on natural history, medieval and Byzantine images of Christ or the Virgin; and enlarged reproductions from works on art and artists of the past, or on original graphics: Gustave Doré caricatures, Zanetti cartoons, antique sculpture, Giacometti, Goya, van Gogh and Rembrandt self-portraits, Morandi, Leonardo cartoons, Egon Schiele and the "character heads" of Messerschmidt; and finally there are the hundreds of drawings made directly on the pages of eighteenth- and nineteenth-century illustrated books. All this eventually crowded into the studio, surrounding the artist who moved, as I said, in circles through all these new motifs. He added experience to experience. Each new motif brought other accents and variations, new twists and tricks into an amazing and expanding vocabulary. Many of the motifs exist only in works on paper; some of the groups are fairly small but some run into several hundred sheets. As a central line, through this geography of expressions, run the paintings — absorbing and rearranging the vital experiences of the drawings.

The studio guarantees isolation and concentration. Some modern artists tend to slip away from the solitary concentration of the studio. Like Picasso or Matisse they move in the world, they move flirtatiously with the world — and their paintings bounce, taking their energy and color from the bustle of cities and the sunlight of holidays in the south. Picasso and Matisse were extremely mobile painters, quick to react, to changing circumstances, energetic, spectacular and full of surprises. But Mondrian was a painter of the studio, isolating himself with his vision and patiently and painstakingly working towards the ideal. Picasso painted *Guernica*: in the work of Mondrian, who fled to England and then to New York, there is no trace of the war. The studio allowed him concentration by shielding him from the world.

Arnulf Rainer, by the middle of the fifties, was working in his studio in Vienna on *Crosses* and *Übermalungen* — and in doing these radical works he decisively extricated himself from the intricate circumstances of his artistic background. It is customary to say that Rainer is an Austrian artist. That should explain everything — but it does not, not completely. The dense pictorial qualities of his work, color heaped upon color, and its curvilinear structures certainly bring back memories of those incredibly opulent Baroque churches — the opulence not so much of the architecture but of the blue and red and gilded decorations covering the entire interior like twisting foliage. Of course there is a historical and regional aspect to aesthetics. The eye and the formal instinct of an artist are first shaped by what most closely surrounds him; that is the aesthetic articulated by local traditions. For Rainer it is almost unnatural or impossible to draw a straight line; the straight line was never part of Austrian art. The Baroque slipped eventually into Jugendstil; and in Austria the notion of modern art was not established by Cubism and abstract art but by the nervous modernists of the Secession movement; Gustav Klimt, Egon Schiele and Oskar Kokoschka, who took their international lead from van Gogh, Toulouse-Lautrec and Munch — not from Cézanne or Seurat. The languid, sensual style of the Secession painters, hedonistic and nihilistic at the same time, coincided magically with the glowing decline and breakup of the Habsburg empire. It was an epoch of inspired decadence. The painting was brilliantly artificial and strangely ceremonial. It was a culture of introspection and withdrawal, obsessed with death and with a predilection for minute detail and for obscure and fantastic experiment; it also produced, of course, Ludwig Wittgenstein and Sigmund Freud, as well as Gustav Mahler and Arnold Schönberg, and some brilliant writers like Georg Trakl and Robert Musil. This too was the background of Rainer — not only the codified and opulent beauty of the Baroque but also the introspective, experimental culture of the turn of the century, which was nevertheless a culture sadly stagnant, without real prospects or spectacular ideals, critical and nihilist and strongly inclined to turn private emotion into an objective standard for life and for art. When he started as an artist, shortly after World War II, it was rather logical that his interest was first in Surrealism. He even went to Paris to look for André Breton. He showed the High Priest some of his Surrealistic drawings but the reaction was cool. I asked him whether he understood any French. He said no, but he would sit in rooms listening to the Surrealists talking and arguing, understanding little but absorbing the atmosphere. It is in the early fifties. He is becoming a modern artist. He meets contemporaries, takes part in avant-garde exhibitions and experiments with methods like automatic and blind drawing. His surrealistic drawings were dark and dense with small figures floating in space, with little internal structure. From there he moves easily into Tachism of which the instinctive precepts originated in Surrealism. The movement is still commanded from Paris. Jackson Pollock is not yet a factor. The masters are artists like Georges Mathieu and Jean-Paul Riopelle.

It was from this background of speculation and experiment that Arnulf Rainer broke away when he began the first *Übermalungen*. As I see it, it was then that he removed himself from the world in which many conflicting artistic developments were taking place, to isolate himself in the studio. As paintings the *Übermalungen* are the typical result of solitary conception and contemplation. In another context he spoke of painting as prolonged conversation with himself. There is something extraordinary about the *Übermalungen*, something hesitant and searching. The working process is cautious and circumspect, like treading in a labyrinth. That slowness also marks their difference from the usual Tachist painting, which in general is quick and lively; the brushstrokes bounce on the surface; brushstrokes play with each other, like dancing butterflies. The surface is multicolored and sparkling. That, at least, is the aesthetic intention: vibration and spontaneity. Rainer, instead, has spoken of mortification and of immobilizing the surface or hiding it under a mute and mysterious veil. The *Übermalungen* consist of painting on top of another painting, either some painting by himself or one of a colleague. There is no record of what image, or whose image, hides under the subsequent, many layers of paint;

and Rainer claims he has forgotten, after so many years. It makes no difference however. Because some *Übermalungen* left the studio in a relatively early state, they carry fewer layers of paint than certain other paintings that remained at hand in the studio and on which he could continue to work. We can witness the process of over-painting in various stages towards "completion" and thus extrapolate something like a method. The first act, it seems, was the rapid covering up (to judge from the broad, quick and agile brushstrokes) of the existing image — the layer of paint starting at one or two sides of the rectangular canvas. That way the layer of paint covering up the existing image did not become an ambiguous second image, drifting in space. The reference to the picture edge established a vital relation to the picture plane. The first, rapid effacing (as if to get it over with) was only the beginning of a process which, in the course of time, it seems, kept slowing down — towards eventual completion, which would ideally occur when the painting, in visual terms, could come to a total standstill. But in the context of these paintings, and, indeed, Rainer's work in general, that notion of completion is very ambiguous. He has often said that he himself is never quite sure when a painting is finished; when he no longer sees any progress, when the painting is not becoming tighter or when it is not gaining in density, he stops working on it.

It could be that work on that particular painting may never recommence. When work is stopped on an *Übermalung*, for instance when the artist sells it, the painting is not consciously finished but terminated. In the case of working simultaneously on various examples in a group of paintings, finishing a painting is avoided and, as it were, postponed to the next painting. Because of their size and the scope of their ideas and the prolonged labor invested in them, the *Übermalungen* (or the large *Crosses* related to them) are generally single works. However, Rainer develops many themes in the form of series — a group of smaller works, equal in size, which explore the range of possibilities offered by the motif. But a single work eclipsing the others does not emerge from such a series. As an observer following private taste and under-standing, one may select a particular painting as more fascinating or more beautiful than the rest. In principle, however, the series is a set of equal variations, intentionally fragmentary, finished or almost finished — or at least abandoned — as they are. The painter himself declines to make choices or express opinions regarding individual works, at least in public. He tends to leave those judgments to the realities of the market and of exhibition-making. Paintings are selected for exhibitions, they get sold and dispersed, others come back to the studio or go into storage.

Thus the sifting takes place. Yet some groups of paintings are only released a number of years after their making — maybe because he is not quite sure of them, more likely because he feels that the particular theme has not exhausted itself. Those elusive, only partially fulfilled paintings he wants in his vicinity, in the privacy of the studio, to study them intensively, to understand them better. The studio is a labyrinth of colors and forms and gestures, a fluent labyrinth of combinations.

After the previously existing image was covered up for the first time, quickly but irrevocably, the *Übermalung* could start its slow and ceremonious growth and progression — from the invisible image towards the monochrome image. Being darkly monochrome is their visual essence. They are virtually spaceless; like icons they confront you.

The monochrome, wrote Rainer, was the "royal road towards immobilization and mortification." He uses predominantly dark colors, black and blue and dark green or dark red. Occasionally there is a brighter red or yellow; but even those colors, employed in the patient, unavoidable covering of the surface (slowly closing like a curtain) attain a visual weight that makes them look darker. Paint becomes heavy, layer after layer, accumulating in a thickening, impenetrable veil. It is painting that submerges everything in a gradually stiffening surface of monochrome paint; painting that relentlessly forces the previous image and previous surface out of its way and to disappear. Yet almost never is the surface covered up entirely. Usually, in a corner or along the edge, a fragment of the original surface remains untouched and visible. This makes the painting curiously hesitant; it is an indication of the extreme caution and, again, slowness with which the whole process is being conducted. Near those areas the previous layers of paint may remain visible: the brush moving along the outline of the previous layer but not quite covering it. Some layers leave some trace. It is the logic of the *Übermalungen* that each layer is slightly different from the previous one. So the thickening of the surface is achieved by variation.

There are occasional variations in color. Sometimes the paint is coarse and dry. The next time the paint may be smooth and flowing — sometimes leaving shiny patches on the previous crust. Like the skin of an old man, the surfaces of the *Übermalungen* are covered with marks and incidents. Brushstrokes differing in size and direction and force of movement. The boldly smearing brush or the brush almost caressing. Remnants of dripping or running paint; traces of paint touching paint. Detail covering detail, incident upon impulsive incident. Impulsive details that give a full and fascinating liveliness to the dark, impenetrable surfaces of the *Übermalungen*. They give distinction and identity to the painted surfaces but they do not reveal their mystery. They reveal something of the long process of their making and then leave them as enigma. Unlike the *Black Paintings* of Frank Stella, Rainer's contemporary, they are not constructed according to plan. The construction or the becoming of a painting by Stella can be followed by the eye. Rainer's *Übermalungen* are not readable in that way nor are they meant to be. They are the last station of painting, left as painting stopped. Unlike the monochrome white paintings of Robert Ryman, another contemporary, they look old. They carry the layers of paint like weight. By comparsion the surfaces of Ryman's paintings are airy and articulated, full of reflected light. The *Übermalungen* absorb light into enigmatic darkness.

It was in the context of the monochrome *Übermalungen* that Rainer, in the mid-fifties, began to use the shape of the cross. The theme of the cross came to an end with the *Übermalungen*, until it reappeared around 1980 in connection with the "chaotic" finger paintings. The vertical-horizontal structure of the cross, he said, was like monochrome painting, a way to arrive at the motionless picture. The usual rectangular painting, if it is not a square, has a dominant visual direction, either vertical or horizontal. For the *Übermalungen* Rainer as a rule used a vertical rectangle. This inevitably enhanced the impression of the layers of paint falling down like a lowering curtain; in some of the works there is a tension between the rectangle of the painting and the painted shape. Just as the monochrome surface absorbs the tension between opposing and conflicting colors, the cross subdues the visual domination of a single direction. The outline of the cross is strong and particular, moreso than that of the rectangle. The cross has a vertical as well as a horizontal axis; and where they intersect lies the immovable center. That is what attracted Rainer. This is indicated by a group of drawings from the early fifties. They are called *Zentralisationen* and seem to prepare the pictorial strategies employed in the Cross-*Übermalungen*. The drawings are made by drawing lines from all around the sheet of paper into or through the center. In the center the lines meet, intersect and cover each other. This process goes on until the center is densely black. At the periphery of the paper the individual lines are still distinguishable, but in the center the distinctness of each line is lost in blackness. Whereas the periphery is vibrant and agitated, with many lines, the center is motionless. The cross can be an upward expansive shape, as we know from the jubilant examples of the Baroque period. But one can also read the cross as a complex of visual forces moving inward — towards the center and then down. That is how Rainer, in almost of all the Cross-*Übermalungen* that I know, moves the paint. The horizontal arm is usually fairly high up. There the painting starts, going inward through the center and then down

— tightening the shape and tightening the painted surface. Most of the Crosses are high and narrow. The paintings are tight and tautly outlined like the standing women of Klimt.

The works of Klimt, as has been noted, are part of Rainer's artistic heritage — forms and formal effects often seen, appreciated and remembered, the local aesthetic that is always around and which may sometimes serve as example or model. Examples are what an artist works with and from which he wants to move away. He uses them. They are, perhaps, a point of departure indicating and clarifying certain directions and strategies. But there are also ideals the artist seeks out and chooses. Ideals outside his direct artistic and practical experience that nevertheless give inspiration and conviction. An artist is pulled away from the models and examples close to him by his ideals. The ideal defines his ultimate and radical artistic strength and quality.

I think Arnulf Rainer's ideal could be the art of Mondrian — and perhaps also the ideal presented by Mondrian of the solitary and dedicated painter in his studio. Mondrian may seem an unlikely ideal for Rainer. But he was once questioned about a Mondrian exhibition he saw in the mid-fifties. Did he understand Mondrian, he was asked; understand what, he said, I was overwhelmed. It is the inward movement of paint in the *Crosses*, tightening them, that relates these works to Mondrian's abstract paintings. Mondrian used his black lines and their intersections to localize and set off color and to pull the color and the white ground together. Therefore his paintings are not just particular subdivisions of a picture plane, subdivisions distinguished by size and shape and color. The paintings carry or hold a lucid and transparent structure that is located *within* the painting. And it is within the painting that the lines and intersections stabilize and tighten the internal space. It is this quality of tightness, a tightness that is open and lucid, which I believe Rainer observed in Mondrian and which fascinated him. What he discovered in Mondrian may have helped him to tighten his own painting — to make it more compact and controlled than the looser and spontaneous Tachist painting that was his early background.

There is an element of obsessive conjuration in the *Übermalungen* and the *Crosses* — like that of some magician incessantly chanting the same phrases and formulations. This obsessiveness is certainly part of Rainer's artistic character — which has sometimes been described as mystical and religious. In his own writings, too, he often emphasizes how much a certain theme may absorb him, almost beyond reason. Yet he never allows himself to be trapped by a single theme. He likes to bring himself into situations that allow for surprise and discovery when his instinct tells him to move on. Thus he began to develop what was to become the next major group of works after the *Übermalungen* — generally known as *Face Farces* and *Body Language*. It is a very extensive group of mostly small works that can be subdivided into several sections, such as works based on facial expressions and on body poses. That last group could be subdivided further into different positions of the body like sitting, standing up or lying down, crouching or jumping. Other themes were then derived from the main groups — for instance, drawings on photographs of female acrobats, or works based on erotic and sexual movements and positions, or a large series of death masks showing not grimaces but ultimate facial expressions. These were begun in the late sixties, but some years before that he had made works on paper that, in retrospect, can be considered preparatory to them. There are, for example, a few drawings on images by Schiele, emphasizing poses and accentuating particular expressive details, and there are several groups of drawings, made in a state of intoxication, of burlesque profiles and cartoonlike heads and faces. To then use photographs of exaggerated and contorted facial expressions was a logical and effective step.

When a painting is large, like the major *Übermalungen* and *Crosses,* it confronts the painter in a way that keeps him at a distance. He has to reach out to touch it. He needs more control to work on it. The distance is not only physical. It also affects the visual experience of its surface. The surface works more as general image than as an accumulation of detail. The painter's visual grasp of small paintings or drawings like the *Face Farces* and *Body Language* series is much closer than it is with large works. He is more intimate with the details. The details are sharper and clearer, more interesting; they demand a different kind of attention. Rainer was from the beginning, when he did the phantasmagoric surrealist drawings, a master of detail. The *Übermalungen* gave him the experience of a different and larger kind of painting. In a sense they are about the elimination and suppression of detail; but even that was done with slow deliberation and detailed care. In terms of artistic attitude, the delicate and cautious amassing of paint on large surfaces is not far removed from building up the figurative density of the earliest drawings. But the *Face Farces* and *Body Language* series are somewhat different — which is why they could so dramatically expand and intensify Rainer's vocabulary and range. Their starting point is not a flat image (to be flatly and attentively covered up) but a photograph. That is, an illusionistic image, a face or a figure arrested in agitated movement in an illusionist space. These photographs were intended to be precise and detailed. It was exactly their function to articulate differences — the differences between very distinctive and carefully calculated states of facial or bodily expression. Rainer has remarked that facial and bodily expression are forms of human communication that preceded spoken language. He contends that they are more complex and richer than speech. They are impulsive, instinctive and emotional. Language is formalized — just as styles of art after a while tend to become formalized. The emotional expressions of body and face are, in their own way, precise and detailed. What Rainer did, in working on those photographs, is articulate their possible expression — or realize their expression. He would contemplate an image and decide in which direction it should be worked over and heightened or intensified or changed or subverted or ridiculed — by lines and colors emphasizing or obliterating or bringing out certain detailed characteristics of the photographic image.

Rainer worked on those images in many different ways. Sometimes he worked rapidly, touching and scratching and hitting, letting himself be led on by the suggestive image without much conscious control. Some images are only lightly touched as if the inspiration had evaporated almost immediately. Other images have become almost invisible, submerged in color or a dense web of scratches and lines. Sometimes he proceeded with great caution and respectfully. Of course the method depended in part on the motif in front of him. Acrobatic movement and erotic ecstasy provoke a different reaction than masks of the dead. Some of the motifs are worked over violently; many of the death masks are tender and fragile.

If he was not himself the one who posed or the actor or exhibitionist, he at least selected the photographs. One has the impression he selected them as voyeur, changing roles, but with the intimate experience and knowledge of posing. He has mentioned the discipline involved in posing for the camera and actually producing grimaces and postures. Of course he might be carried away and lose control — but then there is always the process of sifting and selecting. Looking at the images, after they have been worked on, one senses a certain programmatic line in them — as if Rainer has some imaginary compendium of all the expressions of body and face in mind. His images are all different from one another. The expressions do not appear to be casual. They are not images of chance and circumstance. In their expressive differentiation there is a particular calculation. Each image is a distinct element in the eventual compendium. It is towards that compendium that the series is being built up — in an unremitting practice of variaton and differentiation, endlessly improvised in the manner of a composer looking for new formulations of sound. In this way Rainer has actually extended the formal range of his art beyond the vocabulary of Expressionist and Tachist art. He has consciously used the surprises offered by the *Face Farces* and *Body Language* series to break down his own aesthetic habit

— or to undermine the aesthetic habit of which the "monotonous" *Übermalungen* are, at the other end of the scale, a high example. Because they constitute an adventurous and hallucinatory journey through human emotion and states of mind (from the sad to the joyful, from the tragic to the burlesque), these works are radically new as well as formally exciting.

Because they are photographic images of contorted faces, they are irregular. They depart from the familiar form of the composed face. The body poses are in themselves gestural. Unlike the flat, rectangular *Übermalungen*, these images present many different directions in which lines and colors can go. They are not in repose spatially, they are wild and hectic spatially. Working with this unpredictable and elusive material, with no end to possibilities for discovery and surprise and formal adventure, Rainer realized a group of large paintings on top photographic enlargements of his own farcial face. They were made between 1969 and 1974. They are rich in color and flamboyant in gesture. After the motionless *Übermalungen*, they represent a decisive and fundamental move into a spectacular kind of colorful image. Because they are large, as large as some of the *Übermalungen*, Rainer had to adapt the new vocabulary, which had been tested and developed in the intimacy of the small, detailed drawing, to the grander scale. And they are paintings. Therefore they may look theatrical. They blow up an intimate image of body or face — and then employ that blunt, looming form as carrier or skeleton for the pictorial splendor of thick, curving strokes of color, bizzare patches and streaks, cascades and garlands, hiding the face and uncovering it, adorning and dramatizing. In the tendency to pile up paint, to cover paint with more paint, there is a memory of the *Übermalungen*. This predilection for the fat, heavy surface is characteristic of all of Rainer's art. But the new paintings are not ritualistic like the *Übermalungen*. They are bright and gestural, full of bravura, impressive and amazing like waves breaking on rock, brilliant exploits of painting.

The *Übermalungen* were a single-minded pictorial exercise and adventure. Like the art of many of his colleagues (Stella, Ryman, Yves Klein, Lucio Fontana or Jan Schoonhoven) they addressed in their own way the philosophical problem of the pictorial image — and the question of how, in practice, to construct that image. The *Face Farces*, on the other hand, transported Rainer into a labyrinth of expressions, a chamber with a hundred mirrors, and hence into a labyrinth of formal incident. There is no single objective in them. Their objective is multiple and chameleonic. Straightforward painting is shattered, like a broken vase, into many fragmentary and restless images. The agitated finger paintings are like a noisy counterpoint to the mute, submerged surfaces of the *Übermalungen* — yet both groups are linked by their obsessiveness.

The first finger paintings originated in 1973. Rainer has told how he was working frenziedly on a large *Face Farce* when his brush broke. Because he did not want to lose his concentration, he carried on with his fingers. He liked the feel of paint on his fingers. He understood that painting with hand and fingers (and occasionally with his feet) provided a directness and swiftness of touch that could be another kind of translation of an emotional state of mind into an image. In the *Face Farces* the final image was an articulation of sorts of what was there, as matrix, in the photograph. With the finger paintings he did away, at first at least, with the intermittent image. Instead he gave himself over to impulse: hitting and slapping and brushing over the cardboard surface, working on a number of paintings simultaneously, slapping here and brushing there, looking but not allowing himself to think, working too rapidly to control the image in detail. These seances of obsessive and hectic painting are comparable to his posing in front of the camera and producing grimaces. Now the instinctive acting leaves direct imprints and traces on the painting.

They are extraordinary paintings, inexhaustible in their capacity for change. That there are many of them is part of their changeable nature. But one can distinguish several distinct groups.

At first the paintings reproduced single-minded, abrupt, decisive movements, basically of the flat hand (or two flat hands moving in some sort of symmetry). Compared to the later finger paintings, these first works are not paticularly complicated. Soon certain formal motifs begin to appear. In a somewhat looser manner this had also been the case with the development of the larger, more ceremonial *Face Farces* in which something like a repertoire emerged: crownlike forms on top of the head, plumes coming out of the ears, paint flowing along the cheeks, flowery patches on the shoulders — nothing really repetitive but still somewhat consistent. In the early finger paintings, for instance, the single flat hand, full of paint (usually one color, often red in case the hand started bleeding), forcefully slapping the surface and then diagonally brushing down until there is no more paint on the hand. Doing this with two hands simultaneously produces a V-like shape — and doing it repeatedly in a semicircular way produces a shape like a fan. Something like a bunch of flowers appears when flat hands leave quick, single marks. Apparently the actual activity of slapping and brushing seems to have been an important aspect. The paintings seem to be the result of an obsessive repetition of movements that make them look like archetypes of fingerpainting. Later, towards the end of the seventies, the paintings become more complex or chaotic (*Schmierereien*), combinations of movements, often with the fingers spread, less slapping than soft brushing and stirring in wet paint. They carry many colors. The forms are often thin, streaky, spidery and serpentine, interwined and interwoven. The early paintings are tense and aggressively formulated — movements abruptly arrested. Many of the later paintings are almost delicate. They seem to have been made with a certain slowness. Unlike the direct early works, they are almost as ambiguous, mysterious, enigmatic as the *Übermalungen.*

In the eighties Rainer also began to use the technique of finger painting on other images. By then the technique had developed itself into an extremely subtle and fluent and refined vocabulary. At first the images he used were the emotional opposite of the flexible technique: the stylized or formalized face of Christ and the Virgin or death masks — faces from which life had departed. Essentially he used the technique of finger painting to arrange for these venerable images a cautious mise-en-scène to frame them in paint. Many of the large, painted *Face Farces* had been put in a colorful, flamboyant, sometimes frivolous, scenery. They were agile and spontaneous. But these later paintings, especially the death masks, are grave and full of melancholy. The emotion of the imgage has, again, informed the style of the painting. The painting is not at all spontaneous but circumspect. The images are not, like the *Face Farces,* used as formal prompters. Essentially they are covered with paint. The colors are dark. The forms are the halo, the veil, the cross, the wreath — sometimes, not always, they are only barely indicated and fragmentary. Most of them are paintings in the slow movement of the adagio. In these circumstances the shape of the cross also reappears. The cross was the most glorious and the most intriguing form, the most beautiful form also, of the *Übermalungen.* Of course, most of the *Crosses* originated simultaneously with the *Übermalungen.* But they are also the great summary of that enigmatic form of painting. They recapitulate the artistic experience of many years, giving it a unique and unforgettable form and identity. The *Crosses* of the eighties stand in a similar relation to the previous and contemporary finger paintings. They summarize and absorb finger painting. One can see that they started as finger paintings — but then Rainer began, with the same slow deliberation and calculation of the *Übermalungen,* to paint over the finger painting, covering it with black or brown or dark green paint, leaving an occasional trace of what was underneath, like a sad fragment. In some of them the process of covering and effacing is in an advanced state. Those paintings have gained weight and strange dignity.

They are very different from the earlier *Crosses*. Because they originate in finger painting their surfaces are more relaxed. They have a similar tendency to be motionless and mortified — yet one senses soft ripples in their surfaces, slight vibrations that the tight and forbidding earlier *Crosses* do not have. They are like dark lilies floating on deep water. That is how they summarize the adventure of finger painting, by bending it towards the earlier experience of *Übermalungen*. The great developments of Rainer's art finally meet. I do not conceive of the history of art as styles eclipsing one another, Rainer once remarked. He feels art to be accumulative; what has been painted will always be there, as part of his knowledge. The artist uses the past and adds to it. In that humble conception there is no progress, only addition. Time is not linear. Past and present are locked to each other in a vast circular labyrinth. The entire labyrinth moves with time. The artist goes around in the studio which is an intricate fragment of the labyrinth.

Studio Gainfarn, 1956/57

28

The Great Arch

Franz Dahlem

Eratosthenes (276-194 B. C.), Fifth Librarian of the Alexandria Library, heard that at midsummer the sun's rays fell almost perpendicularly into a deep well in Assuan, while in Alexandria, located almost directly north of Assuan, they formed an angle of seven and a half degrees to the perpendicular.

From the records of tax collectors Eratosthenes knew the distance from Assuan to Alexandria — 830 kilometers. Such was his knowledge of mathematics that from these sparing data he was able to make the calculations he needed.

The circumference of the earth, he found, was 40,250 kilometers.

An astonishing result, and I felt the same astonishment when I realized the significance of Arnulf Rainer's studio. The first painting that made it obvious to me why every one of the works he had done over a period of thirty years validated his own personal existence was a painting of 1953[1], measuring thirty-two by forty-two centimeters, in the colors chrome red, ivory black, uranium yellow, and gray violet. This painting made it clear to me that Rainer, instead of relying solely on his talent, has invented and learned from the beginning.

But the Viennese understood the Son of Gaia to be a figure of legend, took his drawings and made Old Master-like copies of them.

The spell he uttered in *Cave Canem* was this . . .

water a naked box.

What do the words mean: right now, just a moment ago?

INTERMISSION:

It was 1918. The Russian silent film *Revolutionary Age* faced the challenge of communicating to a largely illiterate populace an IDEOLOGY that was entirely modern, that is, right now, just a moment ago. The visual idioms familiar to the Russian nationalities, who were excited by technology but possessed very little of it, were to be translated by means of IDEOLOGICAL propaganda into a message so universal that it would create the impression that *everyone* could understand *everything* — right now, just a moment ago.

Russia wanted to become a modern country.

It was 1948. Every German and Austrian artist was in a German-speaking no-man's-land.
Paris, the cultural metropolis of the Continent, triumphed, set the pace, and disseminated news that German-speaking artists were quite unprepared to receive. In Vienna, Surrealism found a certain audience, and it was highly crucial to my knowledge of Arnulf Rainer's oeuvre that he adopted distortion in his drawings but kept his paintings free of it.

Many artists in Paris during the 1920s took the cinematic idiom of the Russian Revolution out of the context of PROPAGANDA and IDEOLOGY — right now, just a moment ago — and in their megalomania celebrated this distortion as revealing insights into the primal imagery of the human psyche.

Dreams provided other sources.

Psychoanalysis attempted to exorcise permanent despair by means of communication, overlooking the fact that a false image reflects no light,
without grasping the fact that time belongs to the ear.

In this situation Arnulf Rainer met requirements that implied that his imagery would be acceptable without explanation, and that it was.

The visual idioms of the Russian nationalities were inadequate to convey an IDEOLOGY. In his poem "Asia" of 1921, Velemir Chlebnikov wrote:

> Always a slave, but with the home of the czars
> On your sunburned breast
> And a seal of state for an earring.
> Now a girl with a sword who will never conceive
> Now a midwife, ancient mother of rebellion ("storms")
> You turn the pages of the book
> Whose script was a handshake of seas.
> The people gleamed like ink at night

Shooting the czar was an angry exclamation point!,
The troops' victory served as a comma,
And the battlefield was a series of dots
Whose anger was not hesitant.
Obvious, the people's wrath
Contained in the brackets of a fractured century.[2]

Kazimir Malevich was familiar with this visual idiom and introduced suprematism — the non-objective world — to IDEOLOGY.
What is modern about modern art is that it is autonomous, right now, just a moment ago.

Pablo Picasso acted accordingly.

Arnulf Rainer worked on major paintings in no man's land and made his work public from the beginning. In a conversation about Piet Mondrian, an exhibition of whose work Rainer came to see in Zürich in 1955, I asked him:

" — Did you grasp Mondrian?"
" — Grasp him? He grabbed me."

Arnulf Rainer's dark paintings have a psycho-physical character — documents of light. And since color is not an absolute property of matter, images are reflections. The significance of a process of this kind expands such concepts as monochrome painting into kinetic terms:

The dynamic nature of the process proves that investigations are not triggered by value judgments. This is entirely in keeping with the nature of man, who is one form in which matter and energy are expressed.

This is why paintings should be intuited first, and looked at only second.

As Rainer once reminded me, we are all physical bodies. The mind does not test phenomena, nor does it determine them. Determination would be predicated on the existence of an order; for Rainer this implies working not with an aesthetic but with his body.

Rainer has described his development as follows:
"The expansion of my person by means of mimic acting,
theatrical posing, and graphic formalisms led me
to begin contaminating various branches of art that
I had carefully avoided up to that point. Dramatic
plays and ART PHOTOGRAPHY made me sick; the only
things that applealed to me were mental patients'
drawings and the autistic theater of catatonics,
an art form devoid of pseudosocial trimmings . . .
'Art as a means to develop oneself in the flesh,'
that brought me back into the arena after a decade
and a half of devoting myself to overpaintings
(an exercise in self-mortification and perfection).
But this distilled, reduced, gestural visual approach
doubtless had its origin in my period of *l'art informel* (1949-51)."[3]

A rainbow triggers profound, exciting and stimulating vision.

We follow ourselves with our eyes in our opposite number, in a mirror. When we
catch sight of ourselves, we show no feelings; our vision is a strange thing.

What we show we do not utter.

1 See ill. no. 2.
2 Based on a German translation from Russian by Brigitte von Sövegjarto, Heidelberg.
3 Arnulf Rainer, *Face Farces*, Vienna, Summer 1971.

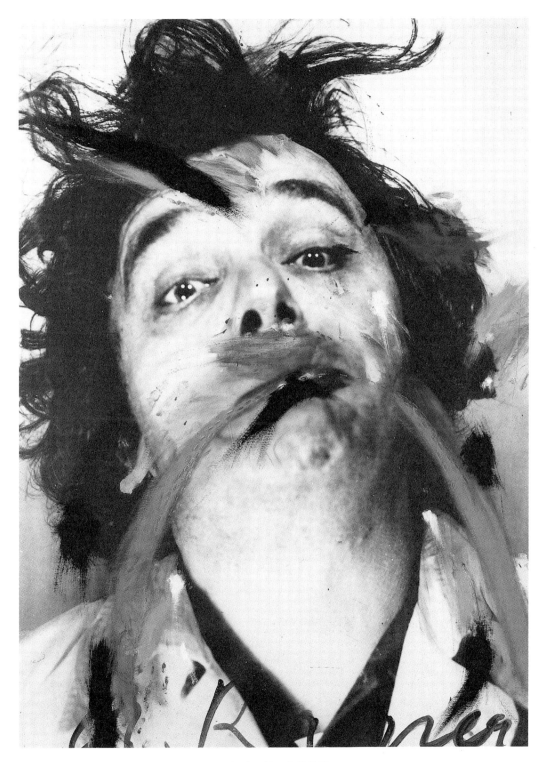

Anxiety (Angst). 1969-73

33

Texts by Arnulf Rainer

Painting to Forsake Painting

Take painting as an example of something that forsakes this kind of world, to unveil its culture and painting through itself, without getting mixed up with the world, unveil it as a substitute for absent and lost metaphysical bonds (where there is neither action nor mission nor evidence nor art), to reveal it as the mere link between the aesthetic and the metaphysical. Be an artist and detest art. For the pictures, poems, thoughts and speeches are foam, yeast, trash, ashes, the absurd attempt to complete the union in the ecstasy (of experience) instead of in a lasting unity (a fruitless method of demand and acquisition). They represent the impossible attempt to prove, the sinful method of trying to seduce by words instead of silence. These are concessions to our dirty soil, we are ashamed of them. Everybody should know, these are traces, not ourselves. So much as an excuse. (1952)

Centralisation. 1951.

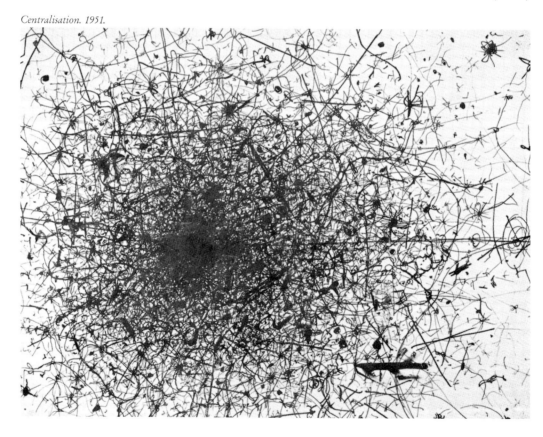

A Single Conditionality

The volume and pathos of the Action Painting of the past evoked silence, equilibrium and hidden things. In addition monochrome as well as horizontal structure (the cross), has proved to be a royal road to achieving a standstill and mortification. Gradually and organically covering up a picture, which should be dynamic, maybe like Mathieu's work, or religious and figurative, is best done with a single dominating color.

The ground of the picture does not have to be by the painter himself. (Did not all the great painters from the Middle Ages up to today also let their monochrome backgrounds be painted by others?) Unlike action-type overpainting, monochrome overpainting is accomplished gradually. For it is a passive creative process, which means the painter has to listen and wait patiently until the next spot to be overpainted makes itself unpleasantly conspicuous. (It is obviously inherent in the structure of each imagination that each point in it eventually expresses this wish, and the sequence is highly important.) The organic creative act might therefore be even more important here than the finished painting, the participation in the gradual darkening or rather drowning of the painting, its gradual entrance into silence and invisibility (the "great ocean") could be compared to the attainment of contemplation in religious life. A single conditionality evolves from movements and acts, a single great emptiness from multitude. The abundance of this emptiness represents the absolute, and the artist must always be the heroic destroyer, because he is the believer.(1964)

Soliloquies
Foreword to a Catalogue for an Exhibition of My Works

I cannot enjoy works of art, for I keep noticing the weak points in a picture immediately, at least when I feel some sympathy for the object. I drift off and cannot manage at all to grasp them. To disguise these weak points, to keep covering them up until I can no longer see them led me to overpainting. It was love and the urge to make things perfect. I wanted to create even better works of art; anything else is just rumor. Since then I have noticed that there is no end to the weak points, even when a picture is completely black, because overpainting creates a new visual structure of its own, and there are weak points again, black in black. So I never cease working on my own pictures. I am plagued by eternal dissatisfaction, while lucky art lovers can still delight in the invisible covered parts. Sometimes, usually in a state of intoxication, I manage to invent some dynamic abbreviation through a blind lightning-fast stroke that I cannot reconstruct later on.

Usually, however, my paintings, even the oldest and best ones, receive one new, generally black stroke of the brush per month on average, so they grow like trees. This will not change until I die. Since I am usually confronted with my own works, I usually extinguish only them. I cannot draw on an empty sheet of paper, unless I hallucinate something on which I can then improve.

I am already afraid of seeing my retrospective in Hamburg, because shame and the urge to improve will seize me as soon as I am confronted with so many of my own pictures that will contain nothing but the challenge to correct them, if only because of the unfamiliar way they are hung.

So my pictures are not there to be looked at, but to be changed. Sometimes that causes problems when they are on loan, but understanding collectors appreciate this perfecting service. In the future I will assure my right to improve by contract.

In connection with the content of my soliloquies during my drawing sessions I must remark that I am usually furious or angry about something. I overpaint to find peace and quiet. There is nothing else that I like. Ideologically, only madmen and insanity have ever suggested enlightenment and possibilities for personal development to me. Seeds of culture in the classic psychoses fascinate me more than contemporary artistic currents. Apart from that I try hard not to produce a homogeneous, consistent art. I no longer exhibit, and have even destroyed some of the works from my extreme phases of development during the 1950s and 1960s since I have no criterion for them. If anybody notices any continuity in my works it is not intended. Maybe my urge to accumulate and cover, together with its dialectic, follows a sine curve of development. That is all I can tell from my past. I understand the single pictures even less. Understanding is only possible for those who have bought them and payed a lot. But nobody has experienced my development, so there is no expert in that.

I am very reluctant to work on pictures or portraits by other artists with whom I cannot identify, so it seems likely that I only want to reproduce myself, that I want to portray myself somewhere in an important part of a picture if not as a whole picture.

Self-reproduction also explains my latest products: photographic documentations of nerve and muscle tensions in my face, and their correction and coloring. This humble branch of art had its origin in the booths of the automatic photo-machines at railway stations. Today, after three years, I have gotten used to the presence of a photographer. It was difficult for him too. At first I had to ring a little bell as a signal for him to press the shutter because the climax of the convulsion, the moment for documentation, could only be grasped by myself. That interfered with my concentration. But everything has a clumsy start.

In the meantime these photos are being sold illegally, because it is possible to reproduce them mechanically. (1971)

Face Farces

When I am drawing, I am agitated, I talk to myself, I screw up my face, I shout at people, I keep moving and changing incessantly as body, character and person.

I wanted to create these side-effects of art to become independent. I had no intention of disclaiming my former products which, apart from overpainting, were devoted in particular to the drawing of imaginary faces, but I tried to leave the sphere of painting. Nevertheless, the documentation of natural mimicry brought me back to two-dimensional structure, especially when I could not help correcting photographs with pencil because I wanted stronger accentuation. I had no criterion like that in drawing when I formed faces. I had only certain means of identification. Later on I strove for familiar denotations again, through these graphic corrections.

During the years 1968 and 1969 I went to Vienna's Westbahnhof train station almost every weeknight. They have an automatic photo-machine there that does not only take photos for passports, but postcard-sized portraits as well. During the day I was frequently disturbed by people waiting impatiently in front of the booth, opening the curtain or even asking to see the photos, when I took ten or fifteen postcards out of the slot and destroyed most of them immediately, because they did not meet my expectations.

So I went there late at night, when the last trains had left and the station was about to close. After I had emptied a glass of wine at the buffet, closely watched by suspicious policemen, I set to work. A certain agitation, an abundance of expression in face muscles and facial nerves was necessary. I had been thinking about it all day long, especially when I was driving through town.

I still practice getting worked up like that, with the help of more or less harmless drugs. Narcotics did not help, they intensify fantasy, but they weaken my muscles.

At first I preferred pictures taken in the booth to those taken by a professional photographer, I did not want a "perfect photograph" and I needed to be alone when I worked. The only problem with photo-booths was to guess the moment the shutter was released. Either I was too late or the camera was. So it was always difficult to document the very peak of tension in the face.

Nowadays I prefer a professional photographer who can take a lot of photos very quickly. I trained us on the job with the help of a little bell I rang. That obviously spoiled the concentration in some of the poses.

Facial tension and physiognomic strain cause not only a formal change of character, an urge to communicate and nervous irritation, but also mobilize those unknown reserves of power that are considered psychopathic.

Acknowledging eccentric structures enabled me to change my personality or rather my face, for I did not shrink from constructing my artistic work on the basis of my psychotic gifts. So it happened in the spring of 1970 during an experiment with mescaline that I became sharply aware of color patches and face corrections on my portraits that were scattered about. I immediately followed the lead of this typical hallucination, and I was able to repeat the psychic mechanism of projection even when working in a normal state.

Since then I have been concerned with drawing over photos of myself, for this gave me the feeling of realizing a reproduction of myself and a symbolic transformation and extinction of myself at the same time. So I practiced self-portrayal, an eternal inclination of all artists, which let me find antisocial inner structures and discover the subhuman in myself in order to make social and marketable products out of these things.

The expansion of my personality through imitative attitudes, theatrical poses and graphic formalisms led me to a certain contamination of different branches of art, each of which I had carefully avoided before. For I do not visit the theater. I detest plays and photographic art; I am only touched by calligraphic marks and the autistic theater of catatonics, a kind of art without pseudosocial wrapping.

"Art as a means of developing the sensual person" — that is what brought me back into the arena after I had dedicated myself to overpainting (an exercise in deadening and perfection) for one and a half decades. Without any doubt, however, my condensed, reduced, gestural-visual formulation began during my informal period (1949—51).

Having become an actor, my future aims are facial theater, published physical exercises, nonsense motion (documented in films) and graphic revisions of myself. There is something I do not wish, though: an audience that is actually present. Apart from that, my inclination to series and small aphoristic, logogrammatic works makes it impossible for me to compete with the American giant-art-mania in exhibitions. Therefore I decided I would rather compile a book first, with the result I had achieved as far.

(1971)

Even Before Language

There must have been a stage in human existence, when people communicated by means of posture, gesticulation and gestures to a much greater extent than today. This may have been before language developed. We know that the primates, especially the chimpanzees, are very much inclined to communicate through facial expressions and that it is possible to "talk" to such animals by means of facial expressions. It shows that there is a foundation in man that has been superceded by a higher rational evolution. This is very interesting, since man is probably a backward being concerning the construction and abilities of his body, and man obviously suffers from this physical inhibition. In general you can say that my work is a combination of descriptive art and fine arts. Body language has always existed in theater and dance, except that it has been subservient to a higher idea, to the idea of roles or elegant and graceful form. These are implications that naturally are out of the question for me, but there are a lot of implications that are much more important for man. There was a very important group in Austria, the *Aktionisten*, which originated in informal painting and tried to make the latent implications of that movement explicit in the language of the theatrical, and through certain processes. Posture and the shape of the body only played a minor role for them. On the other hand, the material and its treatment was essential to them, just as it had been in informal painting. To me the material is actually secondary, and at the moment I am working without any objects, having worked with ribbons from time to time in the past. I am concerned only with physical-corporeal expression. (1973)

One Summer Sunday in 1973 I Was Ready
Gestural Hand-Painting

Once when I was painting over the cheeks on a large photo, my brush broke in the frenzy of painting. Hastily I tried using my hands; I punched and slapped the cheek and was fascinated by the traces of my blows. I decided to use this as an autonomous technique.

I had one big problem though, because I always work in series. My blows were so sharp that after only a few the palms of my hands became sore. Blood flowed into the paint. Protection by rubber gloves was out of the question, so I abandoned rough canvas and chose a smooth cardboard that did not have an abrasive surface, and red paint, so that unintentional soiling by blood would not be visible.

One summer Sunday in 1973 I was ready. With the help of various tricks I worked myself into a mood of concentrated rage and excited determination. The slapping could start. An assistant handed me piece after piece of cardboard. I aimed at each, first with one hand and then soon with both hands, and hit. Soon, though, I ceased imagining that these snow white hard sheets were cheeks. I became fascinated by the shapes of the smears instead, and I identified them as the imprints of the traumatic gestures that my body subconsciously longed for: centripetal, vertical, diagonal. Moving to and fro, bending apart, scanning. But soon they were repeating themselves, and my palms started hurting terribly. After about thirty of these efforts I had to give up. Besides, my studio was full of wet boards. Some of them had already caught splashes of paint from others.

For days after that I was exhausted, and I did not want to hear about these excesses anymore. Without looking at them again, I cleared away the dried objects. It took me four weeks before I dared to inspect them. Half of them seemed to be more concentrated than I was myself at that moment. The others I prepared for a new handpainting frenzy. My sore fingers had recovered in the meantime. I added oil to the paint to prevent frictional heat, for this time I was dealing not with smooth white surfaces, but with unfinished pictures, already smeared and rough.

Only with a few of them was I willing and able to reproduce the old gesture to intensify them. The others called for contrasting corrections with new shades of paint — I had arrived at normal painting, the single gesture was drowned in the object. Again I only kept half of the works. What was I to do with the rest?

41

After another attempt to correct them in the autumn, the pictures slipped into the principles of my monochrome overpainting. Dark shades pushed forward. Gestures concealed themselves completely. But since this experiment of painting with hands and fingers it has happened again and again that I have dropped the brush at a certain stage of nervous agitation, dipped my hands into the paint and applied it with two or three fingers or smeared it with my whole hand, mainly on older fragmentary pictures on which I had not made any progress before. I had discovered a method in myself, I had found a psychic zone in myself that gave me the power to go all out to ravage a better picture out of a semigood old one by an aggressive act of working over and destroying.

As far as pure gestural documentation is concerned, that is to challenge a picture by a stroke, by scanning, by one single movement, I do not feel equal to this kind of concentration at the present time. I hope to have refueled by next summer, so that I can boil and bubble, foam and tremble, so that I can force a picture with a little give and take, a fast gesture of my hands, or even just one blow. (1974)

Finger Painting. 1973.

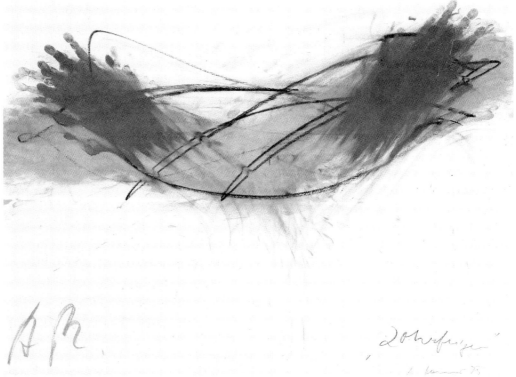

The Painting as Partner
On Hand, Foot and Finger Painting

Born of an impulsive slapping attack on a photographic dummy of myself, painting with my own limbs has always proved a treasury of (transformed) tactile gestures. Gestures like touching, caressing or hitting might be activated concretely as video arts when another person is touched, smacked or anointed; to me, however, the traces of my own fingers on a pure white surface are exciting enough to make me imagine that the hard white rectangle is my lover, whose touch then leaves those traces which are asserted here as characteristics of painting. Naturally there had already been steps toward real touching, caressing, smearing or scratching. I will only mention, but not reproduce their photographic documentation and archiving here. The Southern German expression "I'll swipe you one," synonymous with threatening to box one's ears or to slap one's face might lead some to a one-sided interpretation of this painting. Usually at the beginning I softly touched the painting surface. I only caressed, rubbed and finally thrashed when there was not enough of a sign of life in the intensity of the traces. In spite of this I kept dreaming of soft, fluent touches to create and evoke a pictorial liveliness that reflected strong emotion.

As far as painting with my feet is concerned, however, I cannot conceal here that it only became possible for me when I started to tread on my bad pictures with a productive feeling of hatred or to wipe my dirt-colored soles on them.

Only now and then did I get lost in trivial play with my toes, which I used to make corrections or to apply little dots. Who steps on his women? Caressing has a lot more to do with nails and fingertips, and at the moment I concentrate on painting with them tentatively. However, there are difficulties concerning the support. Even with a good primer, wood or canvas is very rough and soon makes my fingers bleed. For the time being I am using very smooth pasteboard, but I am looking for a, more skin-like support like leather, dried hide or pieces of carpet as a substitute for fur.

In my body-generated painting my interests have turned away from all qualities of color and composition in favor of the unexplored possibilities of direct application of strokes and colors by means of the artist's body. After the broad strokes of the 1950s all brush art became old hat. Rags, stamps, tins for pouring or spraying as tools for painting were quickly relativized. If autonomous painting is still to have a chance, then this chance will surely lie in the consequences of direct tactile-corporeal application that reveals the haptic-physical foundations of all painting. Without any doubt this will lead to pictorial forms that are fundamentally different from those academic compositions in blue which Y. K. [Yves Klein] left and which fascinate everybody who thinks that body-language was introduced into painting in them. Ideas of this kind require full, intense involvement to become realized. Body painting unquestionably produces an imagery completely different from the brush-compositions of the Ecole de Paris. Most of all it is the compulsion to be close to the picture (no extended hand, no extended tongue) that makes the pupils, and at the same time the perspectives of orientation, slide into fearful or euphoric agitation, that prevents the reflection from a distance that is normal for painted compositions as well as for reserved human relationships. No longer to keep the picture, like a partner, at arm's length also means to leave the rectangular format. I have not made up my mind to do that yet, which explains the numerous remnants of composition in my work.

During the last few days I have tried to scratch, rub or slap photo-mock ups of breast, belly, back and cheeks. But I made the mistake of photographing my own flesh, so that only evoked mild emotions and not those passionate gestures of touching that I had hoped for with the skin of a friend.   (1975)

The Completely Dark Picture
Remarks on the Book *Remnants*

For me the *Overpaintings (Übermalungen)*, which I pursued in the fifties and sixties, are the dialectic counterpart to my expressive gestural studies. The *Total Overpaintings (Zumalungen)* developed out of these, through incessant reworking. The original motif peeped through the edges. Gradually it vanished completely. Only the four corners of the background remained. It was terribly difficult to fix my eyes on all of them at the same time. My experience was that the most difficult thing in art is painting in all four corners at the same time. Sometimes I had to force the overpainting of three corners almost without any feeling for shape, almost without inspiration, only to find my way back, to get out of this hell. Otherwise I would have been stuck in this transparent, unspeakable kind of picture. I could only relax when there was just one tiny white last spot left. I could see more clearly. I could grasp the shape of the picture again, I was able to correct it.

The works reproduced here developed in the following way: I touched up reproductions of old pictures, or former states of pictures that I could not get hold of any more, I kept working on them, erased, painted over, covered them up. I did this to improve them, to perfect them, to "mortify" them. I wanted to spread darkness, I wanted an almost seared up black picture. The principles of my works between 1953 and 1965 are the extinction of expression, permanent covering and contemplative tranquility. In the 1970s I took up these principles again in connection with the planning of a book. Realizing that my large early paintings could not easily be reproduced in book size, I felt challenged to create small works that would themselves (without intervening photos) be suited for compiling a book that was an independent work of art. Repetition, mortifications, stereotypes, near-monotony - all that belongs to this series of *Total Overpaintings* and was included in the book. Sometimes the titles are important, because they make an additional dimension of form flare up. Sometimes they only signify what is underneath, or left over or "arbitrary." You should correct them yourself according to your convictions, your imagination, your objections, your superior knowledge.

These pictures are alive because of the white remnant, the almost-concealment, the "not yet principle." It would take more than an entire page in a book to clearly explain this principle of surfaces. That is why I decided to use gray margins.

Obviously they also exist in the original material but they do not occur in my large oil paintings. Adding them gave rise to a new conception of image and considerable changes of form. Thus the original forms, namely the old oil paintings, are hardly recognizable anymore. I might be able to reconstruct them, but the spectator can forget about them. My overpainting proceeds slowly, constantly and cautiously, as I have already pointed out. The great effort making a *Total Overpainting* is split into many small, gradual steps that take years. When I started overpainting pictures of myself and others in 1954, I had no idea that an image that was ninety-nine percent black surface could develop, that this kind of reduction can be realized as a suitable form at all, that it can be communicated to others. This was not a preconceived idea, but a direction developed step by step. My constant dissatisfaction with each black shape and with the imperfection of the surface complex so far obtained was an incentive. Sometimes I was desperate, afraid of losing the implication of the picture completely. Even nowadays I often do not know when to stop, I am not sure if a new stroke of the brush will improve the picture. I often find it impossible to discern the form any longer, I am simply dissatisfied with it. But I do not feel compelled to make a new, important stroke. Whenever I reach such a point, I put the whole series aside for a few weeks. After that I can recognize the weak points more easily, correct more decisively, even see very clearly. Only very few of the people interested in my work are prepared to go along when it comes to the pictures I have covered up to a great extent. Not even the experts in Minimal Art. I feel uncertain myself. But that is a challenge. If I had approval and clarity, I would probably search for different, even more cryptic images. Maybe it is all a chimera, merely the imagination of somebody crazy about erasing, the fancy of somebody seeking nothingness, the whim of somebody tired of the world of forms, monstrosities of somebody morose and fed up with the world.

My ideal is the completely dark picture, full of some overwhelming silence. Only an "almost," a "nearly" is possible. But I have settled down in this border area; I am trying to find distinct standards of shape, and I long to experience, formulate and evoke this dark, heavy tranquility again and again. Constantly starting anew, I try to find variants. The final results are very similar though. Obviously I could exchange top for bottom, right for left. Everything changes in the course of my work. At the moment I favor an empty corner on the upper left. When I am very tired, I want only a bit of white at the bottom.

The pictures that are almost completely (99%) covered are not included here, because when they are reproduced they are no longer clearly recognizable. They are reserved for a later special publication. I hope that one day a publisher will dare to work on them with the appropriate typographic effort. I keep working on this series, which is a lot more extensive than this book. I feel constantly challenged by impenetrability, contact with limits, monotony. (1978)

Blue Black Overpainting on White. 1960.

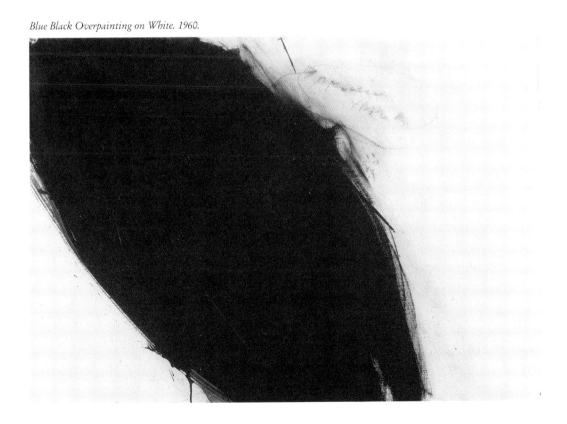

As If It Were Final
On the *Death Mask* Series

The death mask is a document of final human expression. It is the image of an artistic posture; it stems from the completed effort of life to finally express itself. It is the cast of a self-portrait on the threshold of the immediate, the faceless. However, the world of the nonevident is present inside us, because the invisible is the foundation of all art, it is the dialectical opposite of our expressive character, of our impression-seeking, alert life. In my series of death masks spiritual and pictorial principles that have become important to my work in the course of its development come to bear directly (and indirectly as metaphor): extinction, alienation, touching upon taboos, clownish insolence, the quasi-sacral, rapture, curiosity about dying, the mysticism of death, etc.

The search for identification, self-transformation, dialogue and empathy incited me to rework my photos; at least there was curiosity and the attempt to communicate. Dialogue with the spirits of the deceased is an old shamanistic ritual. That is not the reason for my advance toward the subject of death. After ten years of cramped self-portrayal I was especially touched by the imitative and physiognomic language of these faces: having glided beyond, having suffered; interest but no emotion in their expressions. There is no grimacing, no psycho-physical tension, no attentiveness that asks for dialogue; no ambition to make a good impression, no will to distort, no affected exaggeration. Instead of all that there is indifference as if it were a binding form, as if it were final. The countenance of one who has suffered, reached the end of his pain, is free of worries, has stopped fighting, is peaceful, absent and decaying; the frightful and the redeemed appeared here.

The original, more terrifying aspect had usually been disguised by religious or political funeral culture. It had often changed and stylized these documents. So the confrontation with the physiognomy of the dying was made softer, the traces of the agony of death were removed, smoothed out and touched up for a more pleasing memory; the cultivation of an image regarded as more important than the final truths. There are also death masks that were made solemn and heroic, touched up for reasons of political opportunism; there are even deceptive and kitschy death masks made to help ensure the continuity of a dictatorship. Only the religiousness of human futility, Christian ideals of poverty or the disciples of social and cultural outsiders sometimes preserved the real countenance of death for us through authentic immediate casts. Justified or unjustified piety make it almost impossible for an artist, even today, to approach the true face of death, for instance in the medical area. Since I am aware of this, I am waiting and searching and lurking like a hyena to encounter the phenomenon of death incarnate. I frequent cemeteries and autopsy rooms, I collect photos of deceased individuals, I examine the physiognomy of the dying and study mortifications. I want to approach this mystery as a person, and as an amazed person I do not want to brush the problem aside. For me, as for every other human being, this is the great confrontation. As I believe in nothing and everything I want to comprehend religion here. The artist in me wants to grasp it, the designer in me wants to reproduce it, freer of taboos and more directly.

The works that are shown here are only preliminary. There are no great pictures. There are no central keyworks in museum format. They will never really come into being, they are not meant to be. They can never exist, except for my own death mask, the photo of my own death (with imaginary improvements by myself?). A principal work becomes impossible, because only real death can be a significant work. Death emerges as a dialectic background, and it brings finality to any fragmentary achievement in life, and a fragmentary character to any finished picture. Through death anything turns into a provisional attempt. Death is the principal work because it sets the standard. Its physiognomy helps us to understand living faces better. Dead faces qualify past life. They are taboo. We can only endure them when they are blurred or idealized by our culture. I had some difficulties with the custodians of the original material I used here - death masks of great historical personalities. I was suspected of showing hubris and of flouting taboos; I was taken for an artist capable of any violation.

So at the beginning I was never shown authentic original casts. I had to approach the theme via reproductions as substitutes. I had to revise those reproductions again and again, and I had to photograph them anew to get away from the interpreting style of the first photographer. Those photos hardly ever conveyed what I was looking for. After some arguments with the bureaucracy I finally got permission to take photos of some original casts for a very short time. Because of the pressure of time and my lack of experience I did not achieve a lot of important results, however. The opportunity to directly confront the documents helped me to find some new questions though. The faces of death and death masks respectively show enormously different expressions. Is that fundamental, is it a matter of later retouching, or only naive personal projection? The faces of military men, politicians, managers and the mighty seem more lit up, beautified, emptier and flatter than those of saints, great thinkers, artists, etc. This was a different kind of death. Only the original masks of the latter helped me to draw nearer to that special expression I was trying to trace. I would like to ask for hints and help for my further work.   (1978)

Death Mask. 1978.

Lamentation

In 1979 I was able to acquire large studio spaces in Upper Austria and Bavaria, which gave me the opportunity to start an extensive series of *Hand and Finger Paintings*. After placing a large number of drawing boards on the floor of the studio I would move - sometimes crawl - from one board to the other, unloading paint and spreading it across the surfaces. This method of painting could be a culminating point - possibly the last battle - of a creative method accompanied by physical exhaustion based on psychophysical gestural work. The continuous stooping, bending over, kneeling and crawling was a punishing activity - as a result my back is badly hurt and my hands are chapped and sore; only with considerable pain can I now perform certain movements such as genuflecting or bending over.

Doubtless, this will lead to an early end of this kind of work. Yet as there is still a large number of unresolved paintings waiting to be improved and completed - currently annoying me by their silly look - I feel trapped in a dead-end street. To destroy them would mean capitulation. I have forgotten how to use an ordinary paint brush. New techniques using all sorts of new instruments such as kitchen utensiles have failed until now.

Foot Painting remains. Most of the *Finger Paintings* began that way. So, in a good mood, I began to wipe the filth with my feet onto the clean white drawing board. (Sometimes like a summer skier, supported on two poles.) However, this was only the beginning, the introduction. When I changed the position to a close face-to-face encounter with the painting, I experienced the picture's surface as an object of great intimacy. A struggle, or better, a dialogue of love began with all the consequences of great passion. After bowing, stooping and getting down on my knees and rising hundreds of times, I finally remained on the floor. I wanted to be close to the picture's surface. It stirred my feelings and caused excited gestures. Instead of constantly getting up from the floor, I began crawling from picture to picture, slapping and stroking paint on the surfaces. (Having become a "painter animal" I would employ bear and fox paws or tiger claws to stamp the paint on.) Like a chess master playing twenty opponents simultaneously, I would take on painting after painting. I was a catch-as-catch-can wrestler fighting adversaries en suite. Carried away by euphoric megalomania I was convinced I could discover within seconds the weakness of a painting and with a single blow master the picture. Closing my eyes I would launch out with one solitary stroke seeking to conquer the painting. Without looking at the picture again I would advance to the next painting and repeat the assault. Having gone through a whole series of pictures I would get up and step back to survey the opponents lying around me. Yet instead of live beings it was academic boredom that mostly stared back at me from the studio floor. However, when I did like a painting I would quickly put it away and then forget it, so that I could concentrate on those that had not yet submitted - to devote myself to the unfinished, quarter-born creations, the weak and the boring that I had not yet been able to bring to life. Of course it is difficult to retain differentiated criteria of quality in the euphoria of victory. One only distinguishes between what is alive and what is dead, what is strong and what is weak, flowers not yet brought to bloom. The continuous duels and labors of giving birth leave one fatigued and exhausted. Moves and strokes do not work anymore. What remains is ineffective thrashing about, lacking precise communication with the opponent. In this state of exhaustion even desperate efforts of assaulting the paintings but rarely produce interesting forms, unknown gestures, discoveries of new shapes.

A basic stereotypical pattern, a "fan-shape" intruded on me. I discovered it during my painting sessions with the chimpanzees and cannot get rid of it. In addition, another series of trivial motif-systems kept returning. Crosses, diagonals, cup-shapes, verticals, whirls, arches and so on. I am gradually getting fed up with them. I do not like them, but I must make use of them with the strategic hope that they may be elements of transition, anchors in the search for better, solid ground.

Here I am sitting now in my studio, a physical wreck, faced with a mass of trivial, spoiled, bungled, scrawled to death pictures not knowing how to ever finish them, without once more going through that state of utter fatigue and destructive exhaustion.

Can new evolution be expected to emerge out of defeat, fatigue and exhaustion? When considerations, comments, incriminations and self-humiliations make the whole pile of rubbish clear, gloom and despair seize me. How should I get rid of this load of corpses of paintings?

How and where should I bury them? How and where should I burn them?

(1982-83)

Finger Painting. 1983-84.

Catalogue

1

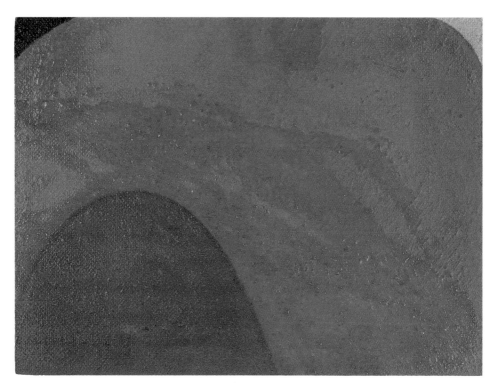

2

3

4

6

7

8

9

10

11

12

13

14

15

17

18

19

20

21

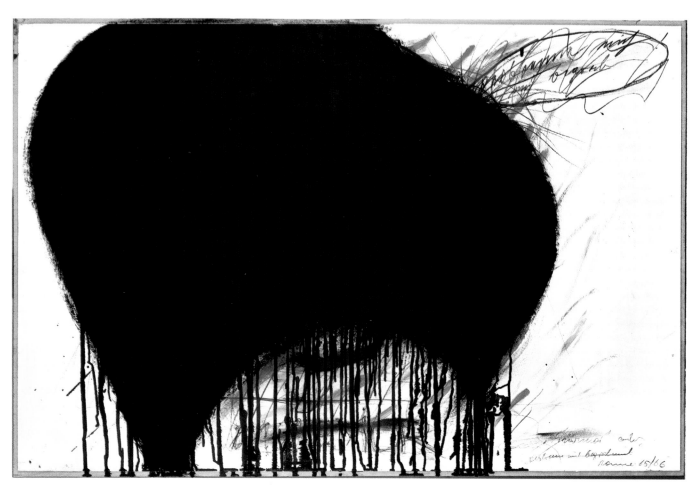

22

23

24

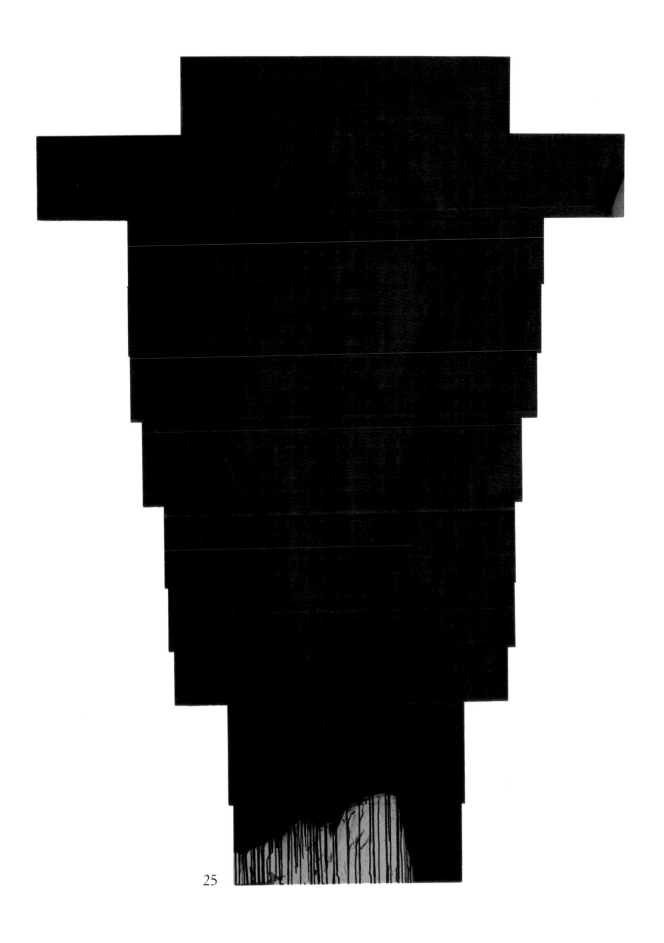

25

26

28

29

30

31

32

33

34

35

36

37

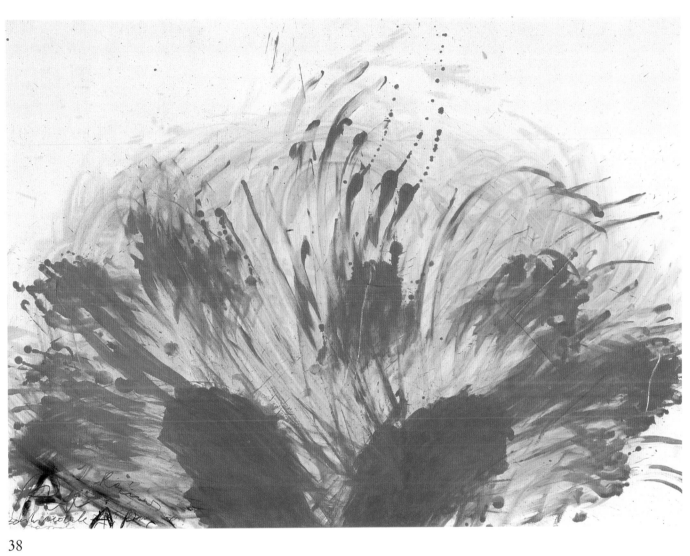

38

39

40

41

42

43

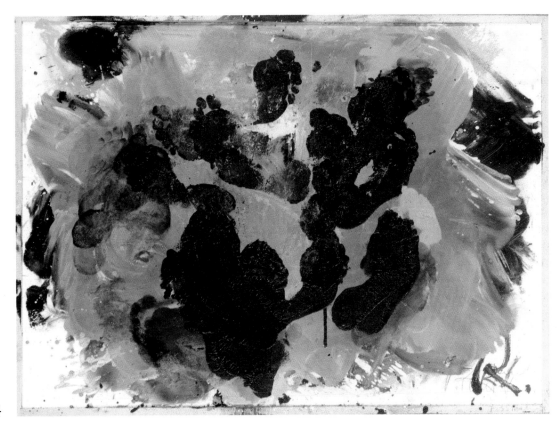

44

45

46

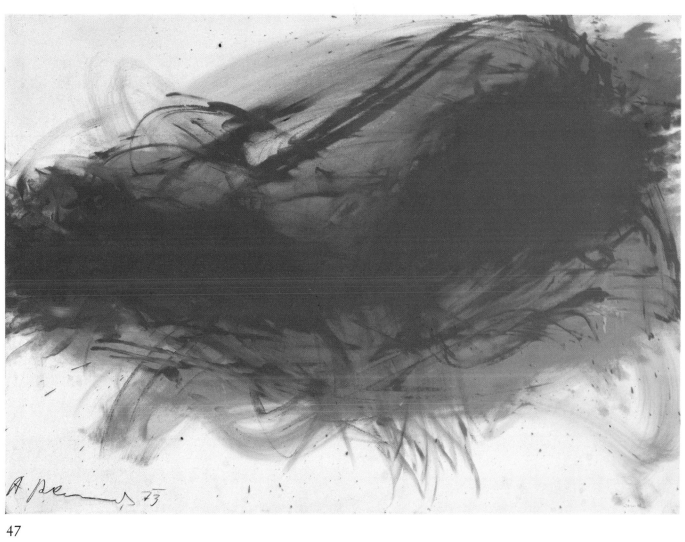

47

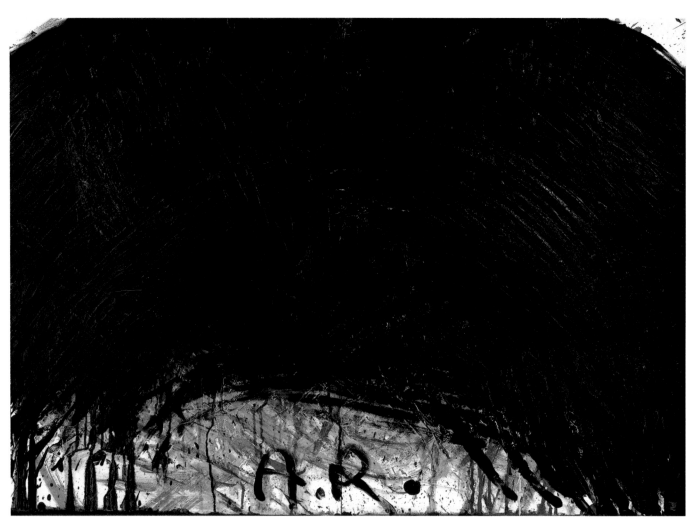

48

49

50

51

53

54

55

56

57

58

59

60

61

62

63

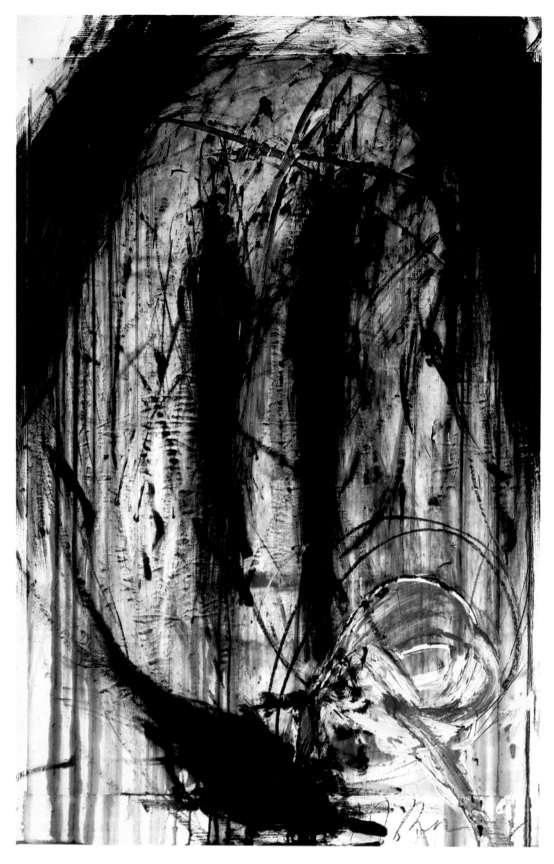

65

68

69

70

73

74

75

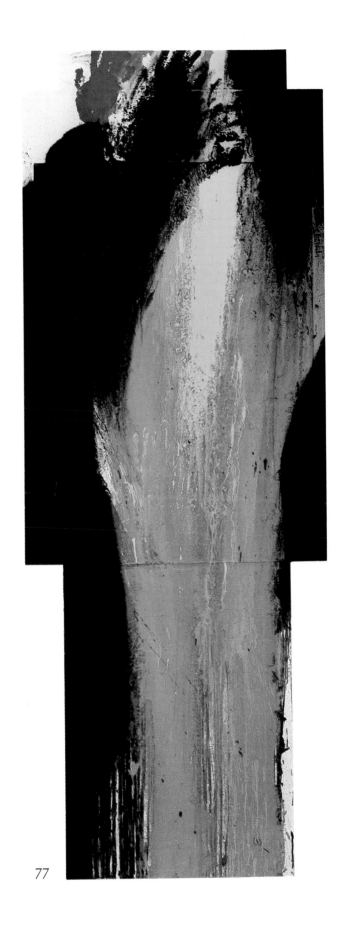

77

78

79

80

81

82

83

84

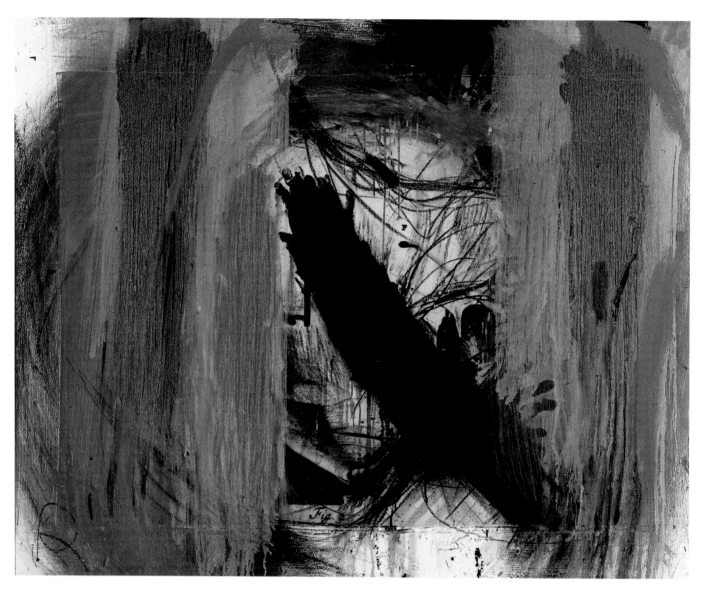

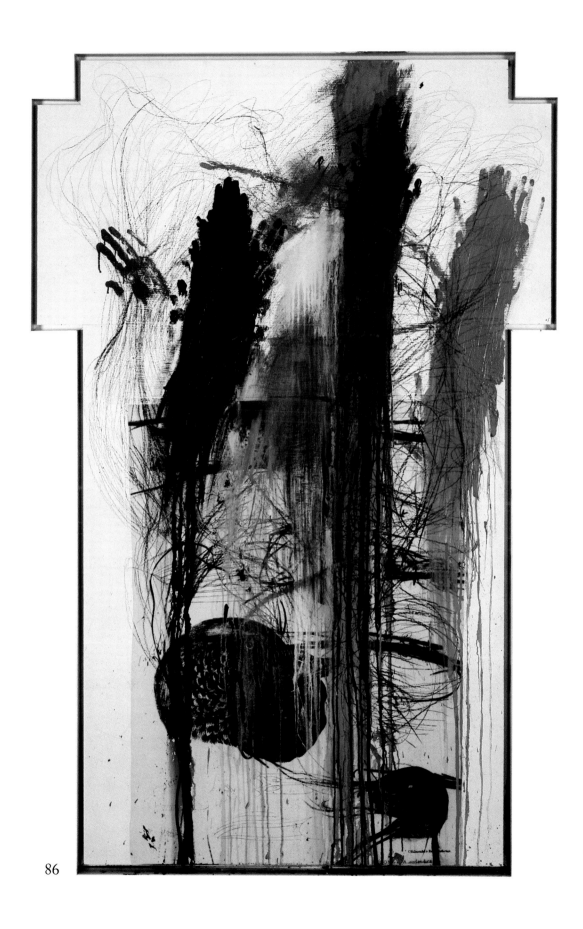

86

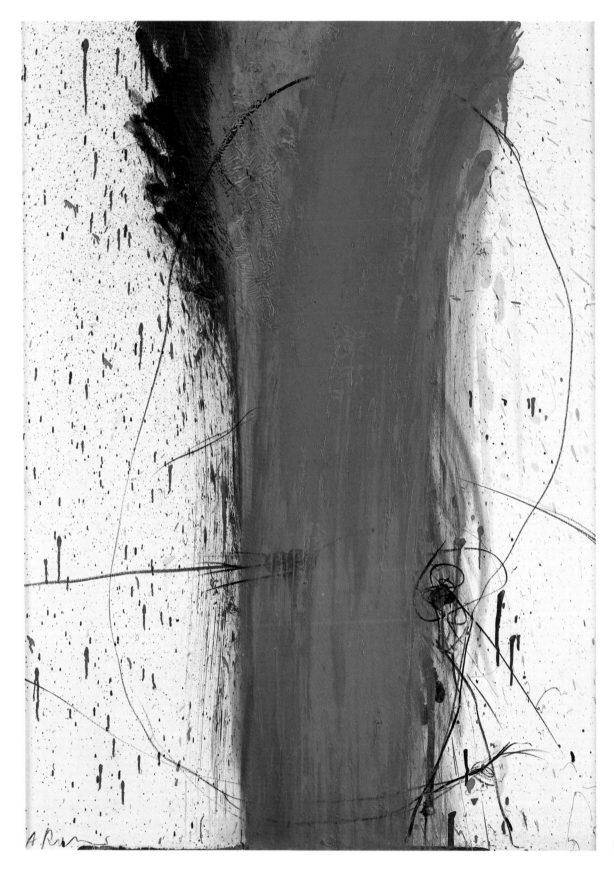

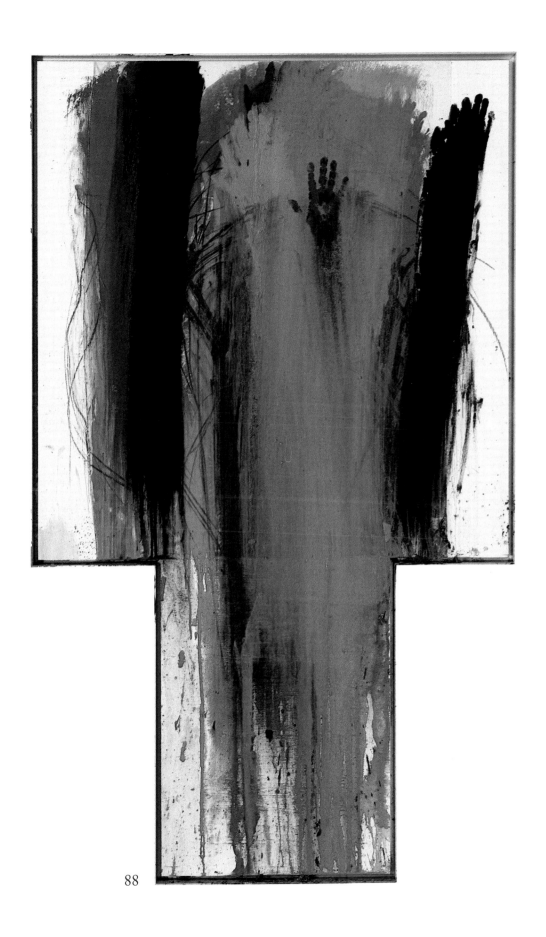

88

Works in the Exhibition

1   *Untitled.* 1953
    Oil on Masonite, 12 5/8 x 16 9/16″ (32 x 42 cm)
    Private collection, Munich
    Ill. no. 2

2   *Full Moon (Vollmond).* 1953-54
    Oil on canvas, 18 15/16 x 15 3/4″ (48 x 40 cm)
    Collection Prof. Unger, Salzburg
    Ill. no. 3

3   *Red Overpainting (Rote Übermalung).*
    1953-57
    Oil on canvas, 54 3/4 x 31 1/2″ (139 x 80 cm)
    Collection Dr. Reiner Speck, Cologne
    Ill. no. 6

4   *Black Overpainting on Yellow and Blue
    (Schwarze Übermalung auf Gelb und Blau).*
    1954-57
    Oil on canvas, 27 5/16 x 41 7/8″ (69.5 x 106.5 cm)
    Collection Dr. Helmut Zambo, Dusseldorf/Vienna
    Ill. no. 8

5   *Cross.* 1956
    Oil on Masonite, 56 5/16 x 45 1/4″ (143 x 115 cm)
    Städtische Galerie im Lenbachhaus, Munich
    Ill. no. 7

6   *Cross Black on Olive Green (Kreuz Schwarz auf
    Olivgrün).* 1956
    Oil on Masonite, 72 1/16 x 59 13/16″ (183 x 152 cm)
    Hessisches Landesmuseum, Darmstadt
    Ill. no. 1

7   *Cross.* 1956
    Oil on Masonite, 90 9/16 x 51 3/16″ (230 x 130 cm)
    Collection Dr. Helmut Zambo, Dusseldorf/Vienna
    Ill. no. 10

8   *Total Overpainting (Zumalung).* 1956-57
    Oil on wood, 39 3/8 x 28 3/4″ (100 x 73 cm)
    Galerie Heike Curtze, Vienna/Dusseldorf
    Ill. no. 4

9   *Green Overpainting with Fiery Corner (Grüne Über-
    malung mit Flammenecke).* 1956-58
    Oil on canvas, 72 1/16 x 52 1/8″ (183 x 132.5 cm)
    Collection of the artist
    Ill. no. 9

10 *Cross Black on Yellow (Kreuz Schwarz auf Gelb).* 1957
    Oil on Masonite, 65 3/4 x 59″ (167 x 150 cm)
    Private collection, Vienna
    Ill. no. 5

11 *Brown Overpainting (Braune Übermalung).* 1957
    Oil on Masonite, 42 1/8 x 33 11/16″ (107 x 85.5 cm)
    Collection Heliod Spiekermann
    Ill. no. 11

12 *Red Overpainting I (Rote Übermalung I).* 1958-59
    Oil on canvas, 51 3/16 x 70 7/8″ (130 x 180 cm)
    Collection Dr. Helmut Zambo, Dusseldorf/Vienna
    Ill. no. 12

13 *Dark Red Overpainting (Übermalung Dunkelrot).*
    1958-61
    Oil on canvas, 79 1/2 x 51 15/16″ (202 x 132 cm)
    Collection of the artist
    Ill. no. 14

14 *Dark Red Overpainting on Pink
    (Übermalung Dunkelrot auf Rosa).*
    1959
    Oil on canvas, 71 5/8 x 51 15/16″ (182 x 132 cm)
    Collection of the artist
    Ill. no. 13

15 *Sea (Meer).* 1959-60
Oil on canvas, 78 3/4 x 51 3/16″ (200 x 130 cm)
Collection of the artist
Ill. no. 15

16 *Cross-Heart (Kreuzherz).* 1959-73
Oil on Masonite, 81 7/8 x 31 7/8″ (208 x 81 cm)
Collection Städtische Galerie im Lenbachhaus,
Munich
Ill. no. 34

17 *Blue Black Overpainting on White
(Übermalung Blauschwarz auf Weiss).*
1960
Oil on canvas, 27 15/16 x 39 3/4″ (71 x 101 cm)
Collection of the artist

18 *Overpainted Crucifixion (Übermalte Kreuzigung).* 1960
Oil on canvas, 98 7/16 x 51 3/16″ (250 x 130 cm)
Collection Dr. Helmut Zambo, Dusseldorf/Vienna

19 *Orange Overpainting on Yellow on White
(Übermalung Orange auf Gelb auf Weiss).*
1961
Oil on canvas, 78 3/4 x 51 3/16″ (200 x 130 cm)
Collection of the artist
Ill. no. 17

20 *Black Total Overpainting (Schwarze Zumalung).* 1961-71
Oil on canvas, 51 3/16 x 31 11/16″ (130 x 80.5 cm)
Collection Kunstmuseum Dusseldorf
Ill. no. 24

21 *Blue Curve (Blaue Kurve).* 1963
Oil on canvas, 28 3/4 x 40 1/8″ (73 x 102 cm)
Private collection, France
Courtesy Galerie Heike Curtze, Dusseldorf/Vienna
Ill. no. 20

22 *Black/Dark Blue Overpainting (Übermalung
Schwarz/dunkelblau).* 1963
Oil on canvas, 78 3/4 x 51 3/16″ (200 x 130 cm)
Collection Dr. Helmut Zambo, Dusseldorf/Vienna
Ill. no. 16

23 *The Waved Picture (Das gewellte Bild).* 1964
Oil on cardboard, 19 11/16 x 25 9/16″ (50 x 65 cm)
Collection Dr. Helmut Zambo, Dusseldorf/Vienna
Ill. no. 19

24 *Fragment (Erwachet).* 1965
Oil on cardboard mounted on wood, 26 3/16 x
39 15/16″ (66.5 x 101.5 cm)
Collection Kunstmuseum Dusseldorf
Ill. no. 18

25 *Forehead-Feather-Prow (Stirnfederbug).* 1965
Oil crayon and oil on cardboard mounted on wood,
27 9/16 x 39 3/8″ (70 x 100 cm)
Collection of the artist
Ill. no. 21

26 *Worms or Burn and Bury Me (Würmer oder Verbrenne
und Begrabe mich).* 1965-66
Oil crayon and oil on cardboard mounted on wood,
34 7/16 x 44 7/8″ (87.5 x 114 cm)
Private collection, Stuttgart
Ill. no. 22

27 *Stepped Cross (Stufenkreuz).* 1968
Oil on wood, 78 1/8 x 56 7/8″ (198.5 x 144.5 cm)
Collection of artist
Ill. no. 25

28 *Large Tripartite Vertical Cross (Dreiteiliges grosses
Vertikalkreuz).* 1968
Oil on canvas, 116 5/8 x 51 3/16″ (290 x 130 cm)
Collection of the artist
Ill. no. 23

29 *Untitled.* 1968/73
Oil on photograph mounted on aluminum, 66 7/8 x
55 1/8″ (170 x 140 cm)
Collection of the artist

30 *Untitled.* 1969/71
Oil crayon and oil on photograph mounted on
aluminum, 66 7/8 x 55 1/8″ (170 x 140 cm)
Collection Ministére de la Culture, Paris
Ill. no. 28

31 *4 Monkeys (The Monkey Family) (4 Affen [Die Affen-familie]).* 1969-71
Oil on photograph mounted on aluminum, 66 7/8 x 55 1/8″ (170 x 140 cm)
Courtesy Galerie Ulysses, Vienna
Ill. no. 27

32 *Self-Overpainting (Selbstübermalung).* 1969/71
Oil on photograph mounted on wood, 29 5/8 x 21 7/8″ (74.5 x 55.5 cm)
Collection Dr. Helmut Zambo, Dusseldorf/Vienna
Ill. no. 26

33 *Hall.* 1969/71
Oil crayon and oil on photograph mounted on aluminum, 66 7/8 x 55 1/8″ (170 x 140 cm)
Collection of the artist

34 *Red Feathers (Rote Federn).* 1969/73
Oil on photolinen, 66 3/8 x 45 11/16″ (166 x 116 cm)

35 *Self-Burial or Christ-Pain, Christ-Joy (Selbstbegräbnis oder Christusleid, Christusfreud).* 1969/75
Oil on photograph mounted on wood, 97 5/8 x 55 1/2″ (248 x 141 cm)
Collection Dr. Helmut Zambo, Dusseldorf/Vienna
Ill. no. 42

36 *It (Es).* 1970/73
Oil with cloth wood and photograph mounted on wood, 48 x 68 15/16″ (122 x 175 cm)
Courtesy Galerie Ulysses, Vienna
Ill. no. 30

37 *Span (Spanne).* 1971
India ink and oil crayon on photograph, 19 5/8 x 13 13/16″ (49.8 x 60.5 cm)
Collection of the artist

38 *In the Corner (In der Ecke).* 1971
Oil crayon on photograph, 18 13/16 x 23 13/16″ (47.8 x 60.5 cm)
Collection of the artist

39 *The End of the Night (Das Ende der Nacht).* 1971
Oil crayon on photograph, 19 13/16 x 24″ (50.5 x 61 cm)
Collection of the artist

40 *Untitled.* 1971
Oil crayon and oil on photograph, 19 13/16 x 57˙5/16″ (50.5 x 61 cm)
Collection of the artist

41 *As a Hen (Als Huhn).* 1971/73
Oil with glass eyes on photograph mounted on wood, 68 15/16 x 48″ (175 x 122 cm)
Collection of the artist

42 *Feathers (Federn).* 1971/73
oil on photolinen, 66 3/8 x 45 11/16″ (166 x 116 cm)
Collection of the artist

43 *New Curls and Tresses (Neue Locken und Zöpfe).* 1972
Oil crayon on photograph, 18 15/16 x 13 13/16″ (48 x 60.5 cm)
Collection of the artist

44 *Raised Hands. Red Stripe (Erhobene Hände. Roter Winkel).* 1973
Oil crayon and oil on cardboard, 28 3/4 x 40 1/8″ (73 x 102 cm)
Collection of the artist
Ill. no. 32

45 *Untitled.* 1973
Black pencil and oil crayon on photograph, 18 15/16 x 23 7/16″ (48 x 59.5 cm)
Collection of the artist

46 *Untitled.* 1973
Black pencil and oil crayon on photograph, 18 15/16 x 13 13/16″ (48 x 60.5 cm)
Collection of the artist

47 *The Throne (Der Thron).* 1973
Oil crayon, oil, glass eyes and cloth on photograph mounted on wood, 48 x 68 15/16″ (122 x 175 cm)
Collection of the artist
Ill. no. 29

48 *Untitled.* 1973
Black pencil and oil crayon on photograph, 18 3/4 x
23 1/2" (47.7 x 59.7 cm)
Collection of the artist

49 *Face Mountain (Gesichtsberg).* 1973
Oil crayon on photograph, 18 15/16 x 23 13/16" (48 x
60.5 cm)
Collection of the artist

50 *Untitled.* 1973
Oil crayon on photograph, 19 1/8 x 23 13/16" (48.5 x
60.5 cm)
Collection of the artist

51 *Untitled.* 1973
Oil crayon on photograph, 18 15/16 x 24" (48 x 61
cm)
Collection of the artist

52 *Untitled.* 1973
Colored pencil and oil crayon on photograph,
18 15/16 x 24" (48 x 61 cm)
Collection of the artist

53 *Red Grease with Both Hands
(Rote Schmiere mit beiden Händen).* 1973
Oil on cardboard, 28 3/4 x 40 1/8" (73 x 102 cm)
Collection of the artist
Ill. no. 47

54 *Repeated Finger Tracings
(Wiederholte Befingerung).*
1973-74
Oil crayon and oil on cardboard, 28 3/4 x 40 1/8"
(73 x 102 cm)
Collection of the artist
Ill. no. 38

55 *Finger Painting (Fingermalerei).* 1973-74
Oil crayon and oil on cardboard, 28 3/4 x 40 1/8"
(73 x 102 cm)
Collection of the artist
Ill. no. 31

56 *Crown (Krone).* 1973-74
Oil crayon and oil on photograph mounted on wood,
34 1/4 x 48" (87 x 122 cm)
Private collection, Austria
Courtesy Galerie Ulysses, Vienna
Ill. no. 36

57 *Backscratching (Rückenkratzen).* 1974
Oil crayon and oil on cardboard, 28 3/4 x 40 1/8"
(73 x 102 cm)
Collection of the artist
Ill. no. 39

58 *Sleep - Spikes (Schlaf - Zacken).* 1974
Oil crayon and oil on photograph mounted on wood,
34 1/4 x 48" (87 x 122 cm)
Collection of the artist
Ill. no. 35

59 *Untitled.* 1974
Oil on photolinen, 66 7/8 x 47 1/4" (170 x 120 cm)
Collection Solomon R. Guggenheim Museum,
New York
Gift, Montedison, U.S.A., 1986
Ill. no. 33

60 *Accumulation (Haufen).* 1974-75
Oil crayon and oil on cardboard, 34 1/4 x 48" (87 x
122 cm)
Collection of the artist
Ill. no. 43

61 *Brown Paws (Braune Tatzen).* 1974-75
Oil crayon and oil on cardboard, 41 1/2 x 30 1/8"
(105.5 x 76.5 cm)
Collection of the artist
Ill. no. 37

62 *Recuperated, Paint Brush over Finger Painting
(Genesenes, Pinsel über Fingermalerei).*
1974-76
Oil crayon and oil on cardboard, 20 1/16 x 28 3/4"
(51 x 73 cm)
Collection of the artist

63   *Dark Footsteps (Dunkle Stapfen).* 1975
Oil on cardboard, 29 1/2 x 41 5/16″ (75 x 105 cm)
Courtesy Galerie Lelong, Zurich
Ill. no. 44

64   *Four Hands on Backside (Vier Hände auf Hintern).*
1975
Oil crayon and oil on cardboard, 20 1/16 x 28 3/4″
(51 x 73 cm)
Private collection, Stuttgart
Courtesy Galerie Ulysses, Vienna
Ill. no. 50

65   *Cross-Hand (Kreuzhand).* 1975
Oil crayon and oil on cardboard, 20 1/16 x 28 3/4″
(51 x 73 cm)
Collection of the artist
Ill. no. 40

66   *Scratch and Foot Painting (Kratzer und Fussmalerei).*
1975
Oil crayon and oil on wood, 34 1/4 x 48″ (87 x 122
cm)
Collection of the artist
Ill. no. 45

67   *Red Backside (Roter Hintern).* 1975
Oil crayon and oil on cardboard, 40 1/8 x 28 3/4″
(102 x 73 cm)
Collection of the artist
Ill. no. 41

68   *Twistings (F. X. Messerschmidt) (Geschlungenes
[F. X. Messerschmidt]).*
1975-76
Black pencil and oil crayon on photograph, 23 13/16 x
18 5/8″ (60.6 x 47.4 cm)
Collection of the artist

69   *The Stooped One Glows (F. X. Messerschmidt)
(Der Geduckte glüht [F. X. Messerschmidt]).*
1975-76
Black pencil on photograph, 23 13/16 x 18 15/16″
(60.6 x 48 cm)
Collection of the artist

70   *Grieving Old Man (F. X. Messerschmidt) (Vergrämter
Alter [F. X. Messerschmidt]).* 1975-76
Black pencil and oil crayon on photograph, 23 13/16 x
18 13/16″ (60.6 x 47.8 cm)
Collection of the artist

71   *Joyful Man with Eye-Stars (F. X. Messerschmidt) (Der Fröh-
liche mit Augensternen [F. X. Messerschmidt]).* 1975-76
Black pencil and oil crayon on photograph, 23 13/16 x
18 15/16″ (60.6 x 40 cm)
Collection of the artist

72   *Finger Smears over Brush Painting (Fingerschmiere über
Pinselmalerei).* 1977
Oil on canvas, 39 3/8 x 51 3/16″ (100 x 130 cm)
Collection of the artist

73   *Covered Woman (Womentalk) (Gehülle Frauensprache).*
1977
India ink and black pencil on photograph, 19 7/8 x
24″ (50.6 x 61 cm)
Collection of the artist

74   *Smiling Woman (Cubist) (Womantalk) (Lächelnde Kubi-
stisch) (Frauensprache).* 1977
Mixed media on photograph, 18 1/2 x 23 7/16″ (47 x
59.5 cm)
Collection of the artist

75   *Planted Nude (Womentalk) (Gepflanzter Akt) (Frauensprache).* 1977
Black pencil on photograph, 18 1/8 x 23 1/8″ (46 x
58.7 cm)
Collection of the artist

76   *Waved Waves (Womentalk) (Gewellte Wellen) (Frauensprache).* 1977
India ink and black pencil on photograph, 18 1/8 x
23 5/8″ (46 x 60 cm)
Collection of the artist

77   *Gray Luck (Womantalk) (Graues Glück) (Frauensprache).*
1977
Black pencil and oil crayon on photograph, 17 7/8 x
23 7/16″ (45.5 x 59.5 cm)
Collection of the artist

78 *Untitled (Womentalk) (Frauensprache).* 1977
India ink and oil crayon on photograph, 18 1/8 x
23 1/4″ (46 x 59 cm)
Collection of the artist

79 *Untitled (Womantalk) (Frauensprache).* 1977
Mixed media on photograph, 19 11/16 x 23 5/8″
(50 x 60 cm)
Courtesy Sabine Knust, Maximilianverlag,
Munich

80 *Gasping (Womantalk) (Luftschnapper [Frauensprache]).*
1977
Oil crayon on photograph, 18 1/8 x 22 5/8″ (46 x
57.4 cm)
Collection of the artist

81 *Untitled (Womantalk) (Frauensprache).* 1977
Oil crayon on photograph, 18 1/8 x 22 5/8″ (46 x
57.4 cm)
Collection of the artist

82 *Death Mask (Adalbert Stifter).* 1978
Oil crayon on photograph, 22 1/4 x 18 15/16″ (56.5 x
48 cm)
Courtesy Galerie Ulysses, Vienna

83 *Death Mask (Georges Baron Cuvier).* 1978
Black pencil and oil on photograph, 23 7/16 x
16 9/16″ (59.5 x 42 cm)
Courtesy Galerie Ulysses, Vienna

84 *Death Mask (Adalbert Stifter).* 1978
Oil on photograph, 23 13/16 x 18 15/16″ (60.5 x
48 cm)
Courtesy Galerie Ulysses, Vienna

85 *Death Mask (Hl. Bernhardin von Siena).*
1978
India ink and oil crayon on photograph, 23 7/16 x
16 9/16″ (59.5 x 42 cm)

86 *Death Mask (Helmut Graf von Moltke).* 1978
Oil on photograph, 23 13/16 x 19 5/16″ (60.5 x
49 cm)
Courtesy Galerie Ulysses, Vienna

87 *Death Mask (Johannes Brahms).* 1978
Oil crayon on photograph, 23 13/16 x 19 13/16″ (60.5
x 50.5 cm)
Courtesy Galerie Ulysses, Vienna

88 *Finger Painting (Fingermalerei).* 1978
Oil on cardboard mounted on wood, 20 1/16 x
28 3/4″ (51 x 73 cm)
Collection of the artist
Ill. no. 46

89 *Bologna Performance.* 1980
Black pencil and oil on photograph, 18 15/16 x
23 5/8″ (48 x 60 cm)
Collection of the artist

90 *Bologna Performance.* 1980
Black pencil and oil crayon on photograph, 18 15/16 x
23 5/8″ (48 x 60 cm)
Collection of the artist

91 *Bologna Performance.* 1980
Oil crayon on photograph, 23 5/8 x 18 15/16″ (60 x
48 cm)
Collection of the artist

92 *On the Carpet in Bologna (Auf dem Teppich in Bologna).*
1980
Oil crayon on photograph, 23 5/8 x 18 15/16″ (60 x
48 cm)
Collection of the artist

93 *Bologna Performance.* 1980
India ink, black pencil and oil crayon on photograph,
18 15/16 x 23 5/8″ (48 x 60 cm)
Collection of the artist

94 *Carpet Scene (Teppichszene).* 1980
Black pencil, oil crayon and oil on photograph,
18 15/16 x 23 5/8″ (48 x 60 cm)
Collection of the artist

95 *Bologna Performance.* 1980
Black pencil on photograph, 18 15/16 x 23 5/8″ (48 x
60 cm)
Collection of the artist

96 *Bologna Performance.* 1980
Oil crayon on photograph, 18 15/16 x 23 5/8″ (48 x 60 cm)
Collection of the artist

97 *Bologna Performance.* 1980
Oil crayon on photograph, 18 15/16 x 23 5/8″ (48 x 60 cm)
Collection of the artist

98 *Cross Painting.* 1980-85
Oil on wood with painted metal, 79 1/8 x 31 1/2″ (201 x 80 cm)
Collection, The Museum of Modern Art, New York
Gift of Mr. and Mrs. Ronald S. Lauder
Ill. no. 78

99 *Cross.* 1980-86
Oil on wood, 67 5/16 x 47 5/8″ (171 x 121 cm)
Courtesy Galerie Ulysses, Vienna
Ill. no. 79

100 *Cross.* 1980-86
Oil with crucifix on wood, 83 1/2 x 31 1/2″ (212 x 80 cm)
Collection Dr. Helmut Zambo, Dusseldorf/Vienna
Ill. no. 79

101 *Crow or Eagle (Krähe oder Adler).* 1981
Oil crayon and oil on cardboard, 20 1/16 x 28 3/4″ (51 x 73 cm)
Courtesy **m** Bochum, Galerie für Film, Foto, Neue Konkrete Kunst und Video, Bochum
Ill. no. 49

102 *Branches (Äste).* 1981
Oil on cardboard, 28 3/4 x 20 1/16″ (73 x 51 cm)
Courtesy **m** Bochum, Galerie für Film, Foto, Neue Konkrete Kunst und Video, Bochum
Ill. no. 52

103 *Finger-Color-Feast (Fingerfarbfest).* 1981
Oil on cardboard, 28 3/4 x 40 1/8″ (73 x 102 cm)
Courtesy Galerie Lelong, Zurich
Ill. no. 51

104 *Finger-Color-Feast (Fire) (Fingerfarbfest [Feuer]).* 1981
Oil crayon and oil on cardboard, 28 3/4 x 40 1/8″ (73 x 102 cm)
Courtesy Galerie Lelong, Zurich
Ill. no. 54

105 *Untitled.* 1981
Oil on cardboard, 28 3/4 x 40 1/8″ (73 x 102 cm)
Collection Kommerzialrat Karlheinz Essl, Klosterneuburg, Austria
Ill. no. 48

106 *Untitled.* 1981-83
Oil crayon and oil on cardboard, 28 3/4 x 40 1/8″ (73 x 102 cm)
Collection of the artist
Ill. no. 59

107 *Untitled.* 1981-83
Oil on cardboard, 28 3/4 x 40 1/8″ (73 x 102 cm)
Courtesy Galerie Ulysses, Vienna
Ill. no. 58

108 *Untitled.* 1981-83
Oil on cardboard, 49 3/16 x 32 11/16″ (125 x 83 cm)
Private collection, Federal Republic of Germany
Courtesy Turske & Turske AG, Zurich
Ill. no. 61

109 *Untitled.* 1981-83
Oil crayon and oil on cardboard, 28 3/4 x 40 1/8″ (73 x 102 cm)
Collection Stedelijk Van Abbemuseum, Eindhoven, The Netherlands
Ill. no. 57

110 *Untitled.* 1981-83
Oil on cardboard, 28 3/4 x 40 1/8″ (73 x 102 cm)
Courtesy Galerie Ulysses, Vienna
Ill. no. 53

111 *Suture (Naht).* 1981-84
Oil and mixed media on cardboard, 20 1/16 x 28 3/4″ (51 x 73 cm)
Collection Dr. Dr. h. c. G. Schomburg
Ill. no. 55

112 *Yellow Skytrain (Gelber Himmelszug).*
1982
Oil crayon and oil on cardboard, 20 1/16 x 28 3/4″
(51 x 73 cm)
Private collection, Stuttgart
Courtesy Galerie Ulysses, Vienna
Ill. no. 56

113 *Prayed, Bent (Gebetenes, Gebogenes).*
1982
Oil on cardboard, 28 3/4 x 40 1/8″ (73 x 102 cm)
Collection Kranz, Dusseldorf
Ill. no. 60

114 *Cross.* 1982-83
Oil on paper mounted on wood, 47 1/4 x 31 1/2″
(120 x 80 cm)
Collection Dr. Helmut Zambo, Dusseldorf/Vienna
Ill. no. 62

115 *Untitled.* 1983-84
Oil crayon and oil on photograph mounted on wood,
47 1/4 x 31 1/2″ (120 x 80 cm)
Collection of the artist
Ill. no. 74

116 *Box on the Ears (Ohrfeigen).* 1983-84
Oil crayon and oil on photograph mounted on wood,
47 5/8 x 31 1/2″ (121 x 80 cm)
Collection Mr. and Mrs. William Hokin, Chicago
Ill. no. 67

117 *Black Dagger (Schwarzer Dolch).* 1983-84
Pencil and oil on cardboard, 28 7/8 x 40 1/8″
(73.3 x 102 cm)
Collection of the artist
Ill. no. 75

118 *The Cultivated Eye (Das gebildete Auge).*
1983-84
Oil crayon and oil on photograph mounted on wood,
47 1/4 x 31 1/2″ (120 x 80 cm)
Collection Austria Tabak, Vienna
Ill. no. 68

119 *Untitled.* 1983-84
Oil crayon and oil on cardboard, 40 1/8 x 28 3/4″
(102 x 73 cm)
Courtesy Galerie Lelong, Zurich
Ill. no. 73

120 *Hidden Face of Christ
(Verstecktes Christusgesicht).*
1983-84
Oil crayon and oil on photograph mounted on wood,
47 1/4 x 31 1/2″ (120 x 80 cm)
Courtesy Galerie Ulysses, Vienna
Ill. no. 66

121 *Death Mask (Ludwig van Beethoven).*
1984
Oil crayon and oil on photograph mounted on wood,
47 1/4 x 31 1/2″ (120 x 80 cm)
Courtesy Galerie Ulysses, Vienna
Ill. no. 72

122 *Tree and Cloud (Baum und Wolke).* 1984
Oil crayon and oil on cardboard, 20 1/4 x 28 15/16″
(51.5 x 73.5 cm)
Private collection, Zug/Switzerland
Ill. no. 69

123 *Death Mask (Ludwig van Beethoven).* 1984
Oil crayon and oil on photograph mounted on wood,
47 1/4 x 31 1/2″ (120 x 80 cm)
Courtesy Galerie Ulysses, Vienna

124 *Death Mask (Gustav Mahler).* 1984
Oil crayon and oil on photograph mounted on wood,
47 1/4 x 31 1/2″ (120 x 80 cm)
Courtesy Galerie Ulysses, Vienna
Ill. no. 64

125 *Death Mask (Franz Grillparzer).* 1984
Oil crayon and oil on photograph mounted on wood,
47 1/4 x 31 1/2″ (120 x 80 cm)
Private collection, Vienna
Courtesy Galerie Ulysses, Vienna
Ill. no. 71

126 *Death Mask (Maximilien Robespierre).* 1984
Oil crayon and oil on photograph mounted on wood,
47 1/4 x 31 1/2″ (120 x 80 cm)
Courtesy Galerie Ulysses, Vienna

127 *Death Mask (Marie von Ebner-Eschenbach).* 1984
Oil crayon and oil on photograph mounted on wood,
47 1/4 x 31 1/2″ (120 x 80 cm)
Courtesy Galerie Ulysses, Vienna
Ill. no. 65

128 *Death Mask (Hl. Johannes Pignatelli).* 1984
Oil crayon and oil on photograph mounted on wood,
47 1/4 x 31 1/2″ (120 x 80 cm)
Courtesy Galerie Ulysses, Vienna

129 *Death Mask (Franz List).* 1984
Oil crayon and oil on photograph mounted on wood,
47 1/4 x 31 1/2″ (120 x 80 cm)
Courtesy Galerie Ulysses, Vienna
Ill. no. 63

130 *Death Mask (Joseph Haydn).* 1984
Oil crayon and oil on photograph mounted on wood,
31 1/2 x 47 1/4″ (80 x 120 cm)
Courtesy Galerie Ulysses, Vienna
Ill. no. 70

131 *The Black Blood of the Cross (Das schwarze Blut des
Kreuzes).* 1984-85
Oil crayon and oil on photograph on cardboard
mounted on wood, 40 1/8 x 28 7/8″ (102 x 73.3 cm)
Collection of the artist
Ill. no. 76

132 *Untitled.* 1985-87
Oil crayon and oil on cardboard mounted on wood,
40 1/8 x 28 3/4″ (102 x 73 cm)
Collection of the artist

133 *Untitled.* 1985-87
Oil on cardboard mounted on wood, 28 3/4 x 40 1/8″
(73 x 102 cm)
Collection of the artist

134 *Untitled.*
Oil crayon and oil on cardboard mounted on wood,
28 3/4 x 40 1/8″ (73 x 102 cm)
Collection of the artist

135 *The Circling Mountain (Der kreisende Berg).* 1986
Oil crayon and oil on reproduction mounted on wood,
40 1/8 x 49 5/8″ (102 x 126 cm)
Courtesy Galerie Lelong, Zurich
Ill. no. 84

136 *Cannibalia Ill.* 1986
Oil crayon and oil on reproduction mounted on wood,
40 1/8 x 49 5/8″ (102 x 126 cm)
Private collection, Lausanne
Courtesy Galerie Lelong, Zurich
Ill. no. 85

137 *Untitled.* 1986-87
Oil on cardboard mounted on wood, 23 5/8 x 31 1/2″
(60 x 80 cm)
Collection of the artist
Ill. no. 81

138 *Cross.* 1987-88
Oil on cardboard mounted on wood, 83 1/2 x 31 1/2″
(212 x 80 cm)
Collection The Prince of Schwarzenberg, Vienna
Ill. no. 77

139 *Cross.* 1987-88
Oil wood, 82 1/4 x 49 1/2″ (209 x 126 cm)
Collection Kossdorff, Vienna
Ill. no. 88

140 *Cross.* 1987-88
Oil crayon and oil on photograph mounted on wood,
73 5/8 x 47 1/4″ (187 x 120 cm)
Collection of the artist
Ill. no. 86

Chronology

1929   Arnulf Rainer is born in Baden, a town twenty miles south of Vienna.

1937   Praised by a teacher for drawing the nicest trees and branches during art class, Rainer experiences the feeling of being an artist.

1940-44   Attends boarding school in Traiskirchen, Lower Austria.

1944   Leaves school because he is told to draw from nature; decides he wants to be an artist.

1945   Travels to Carinthia (the southernmost province of Austria); paints watercolors of deserted landscapes.

1947   First exposure to international contemporary art, through reproductions of the work of Paul Nash, Francis Bacon, Stanley Spencer and Henry Moore in a magazine published by the British Council, London.

1947-49   Attends technical school in Villach, Carinthia.

1948   Discovers Surrealist theories, which have considerable influence on his work.

1949   Graduates from school in Villach. Accepted by the Hochschule für Angewandte Kunst, Vienna; after a dispute with a teacher on the first day, Rainer leaves the institution. He subsequently applies to and is accepted by the Akademie der Bildenden Künste, Vienna, which he attends for three days and likewise leaves.

1950   Meets Ernst Fuchs, Anton Lehmden and Arik Brauer, as well as Wolfgang Hollegha and Josef Mikl. These artist form the *Hundsgruppe* (Dog's Group).

1951   At the opening of an exhibition of the *Hundsgruppe* in Vienna, Rainer insults the audience. Soon after the exhibition, rejects the fantastic Surrealist style in which he had been working and becomes interested in microstructures and destruction of shapes, and produces *Optical Decentralization* drawings, featuring organic structures without centers. Travels to Paris, visits André Breton; is disappointed by the meeting. Is impressed, however, by the exhibition *Véhémences confrontées* at Galerie Nina Dausset in which Willem de Kooning, Georges Mathieu, Jackson Pollock and Jean-Paul Riopelle are represented. Publishes portfolio *Perspektiven der Vernichtung* (Perspectives of Destruction). His last *Optical Decentralization* drawings are so densely covered with lines that they become almost solid black surfaces. Rainer seeks new approaches to painting in order to move beyond this phase: works with eyes closed, creating *Blindmalerei (Blind Paintings)* and automatic paintings. These lead to his series of *Zentralisationen (Centralizations)*.

1953-59   Meets Roman Catholic priest, Monsignore Otto Mauer, who, in 1955 establishes Galerie nächst St. Stephan in Vienna, which remains Austria's most influential avant-garde gallery until the late sixties. Rainer shows with St. Stephan from 1956 to 1970. Retreats to a house in Gainfarn, in the country twenty-five miles south of Vienna. He explores problems of proportion and division. In 1953-54 collaborates with a photographer on the first *Photoposen (Photo-Poses)* of himself. Begins lifelong study of mysticism; becomes interested in the idea of erasing and effacing existing art. Beginning in 1953 and continuing until 1964 Rainer executes possibly his best-known works, the *Übermalungen (Overpaintings)* series, in which he covers paintings by himself and other artists with coats of monochrome paint. (As early as 1951 he had produced nearly monochromatic surfaces in some of the microstructure drawings. In 1956-57 executes series of approximately fifteen cross-shaped paintings (made on Masonite) covered with monochrome paint.

1959-64   While continuing to paint monochrome pictures, Rainer searches for new forms; he creates these through automatic drawings, executed primarily with oil crayons, tracing and retracing lines until the surfaces of the works are covered.

Sam Francis, Emilio Vedova, Mathieu and Victor Vasarely volunteer to contribute paintings for Rainer to paint over.

Participates in *Monochrome Malerei* exhibition at Städtisches Museum, Leverkusen.

From 1964 works in various studios in Berlin, Munich and Cologne.

In 1964 begins experiments with hallucinatory drugs.

1968   First *Face Farce* photos.

Retrospective at Museum des 20. Jahrhunderts, Vienna.

1969   Increasingly explores various aspects of body language; poses for photographs of himself (grimaces and body poses), on which he draws to emphasize certain expressions. These self-portraits constitute an important part of Rainer's oeuvre.

1970   From this date executes numerous series of drawings and paintings on photographs such as *Frauenposen (Women Poses), Kunst auf Kunst (Art on Art) (Overpaintings* and *Overdrawings* of reproductions of works by van Gogh, Rembrandt, Messerschmidt and others), *Totenmasken (Death Masks)* and *Leichengesichter (Corpse Faces)*.

1971   First retrospective in Germany, at Kunstverein Hamburg; participates in São Paulo Bienal.

1973   Makes gestural *Handmalerei (Hand Paintings)* and *Fingermalerei (Finger Paintings)*.

1977   Increasing preoccupation with themes of death begins, as revealed in photo series of *Totenmasken, Leichengesichter* and *Mumien (Mummies)*.

1978   Participates in Venice Biennale.

1980   Acquires large studios in Upper Austria and Bavaria and resumes making the *Handmalerei* and *Fingermalerei*; twenty of these works are shown at *Documtena 7* in Kassel in 1982.

Returns to the religious theme of the Cross in the *Kreuz (Cross)* series of oils.

1981   Appointed professor at the Akademie der Bildenden Künste, Vienna, receives Max Beckmann prize of the city of Frankfurt and becomes member of the Akademie der Künste, Berlin.

Works on series of photographs of crucifixions and wood carvings of Christ.

Major retrospective at Nationalgalerie, Berlin, which travels to Baden-Baden, Bonn and Vienna.

1982   Completes *Hiroshima* series, drawings on photographs of the destroyed city. The series is shown in seventeen European museums.

1983   Continues series of large *Kreuz* and *Totenmasken* paintings.

1984   *Mort et sacrifice,* major retrospective at Musée National d'Art Moderne, Centre Georges Pompidou, Paris. Participates in *Overture,* opening exhibition of Castello di Rivoli, Turin.

Bavarian television produces a film on the artist.

1985   Becomes interested in eighteenth-century books on natural history with botanical and zoological illustrations, on which he executes *Overdrawings* and *Overpaintings*.

1986   *Self Portraits* show circulates in the United States; major one-man exhibition at Abbazia di San Gregorio, Venice. Solomon R. Guggenheim Museum, New York, acquires a large *Face Farce*.

1987   A *Kreuz* painting enters the collection of The Museum of Modern Art, New York. Participates in *The Spiritual in Art: Abstract Painting 1890-1985* and *Avant-Garde in the Eighties* at Los Angeles County Museum of Art. Works on *Overdrawings* of Piranesi engravings.

1988   Develops interest in Shakespearean themes.

Important paintings from Northrhine-Westphalian collections are shown at the Krefelder Kunstmuseen and in Kassel.

1989   Receives award from the International Center of Photography, New York, for his work as a visual artist who has made important use of photography together with other media.

Currently lives in Upper Austria, Bavaria and Vienna, where he teaches at the Akademie der Bildenden Künste.

Selected One-Man Exhibitions

1951 Galerie Kleinmayr, Klagenfurt, Austria

1952 Galerie Springer, Berlin
Galerie Franck, Frankfurt

1954 Galerie Würthle, Vienna. Catalogue with text by the artist

1956 Galerie nächst St. Stephan, Vienna

1957 Wiener Secession, Vienna

1961 Galleria del Cavallino, Venice. Catalogue with text by Werner Hofmann

1962 Galerie Schmela, Dusseldorf
Minami Gallery, Tokyo. Catalogue with text by Pierre Restany

1964 Galerie Springer, Berlin. Catalogue with text by the artist

1968 Museum des 20. Jahrhunderts, Vienna. Catalogue with texts by Werner Hofmann, Pierre Restany and the artist

1969 Galerie Ariadne, Vienna. Catalogue with texts by Otto Breicha, Michael Guttenbrunner, Wolfgang Kudrnofsky, Maria Lassnig and Reinhard Priessnitz

1970 Kunstverein Freiburg, Germany. Catalogue with text by the artist
Galerie Van de Loo, Munich
Galerie Müller, Stuttgart and Cologne

1971 Kunstverein Hamburg. Catalogue with texts by Werner Hofmann, Hermann Kern and the artist
São Paulo Bienal

1972 Busch-Reisinger Museum, Harvard University, Cambridge, Massachusetts

1973 Graphische Sammlung Albertina, Vienna

1974 Kunstverein Bremerhaven. Catalogue with text by Dietrich Helms
Kunstraum Munich. Catalogue with texts by Hermann Kern and the artist

1975 Hessisches Landesmuseum, Darmstadt. Catalogue with text by Hans Schmidt. Traveled to Kunstverein Mannheim
Galerie Stadler, Paris

1976 Neue Galerie der Stadt Linz, Austria. Catalogue with texts by Peter Baum and the artist
Galerie Van de Loo, Munich

1977 Kunstraum, Munich. Catalogue with texts by Hermann Kern, Friedrich Nicolai and the artist
Kunsthalle Bern. Catalogue with texts by Franz Dahlem, Johannes Gachnang, Wolfgang Hartmann and Armin Zweite. Traveled to Städtische Galerie im Lenbachhaus, Munich; with Kunstraum Munich exhibition (see above) to Kestner Gesellschaft, Hannover. Catalogue with texts by Dahlem, Gachnang, Carl Haenlein, Hartmann, Hermann Kern, Wieland Schmied, Zweite and the artist

1978 Venice Biennale, Austrian Pavilion. Catalogue with texts by Werner Hofmann, Hans Hollein and the artist
Österreichische Galerie, Vienna. Catalogue with texts by Hans Aurenhammer and the artist. Traveled to Kunstverein, Frankfurt am Main; Galerie Zwirner, Cologne; Galerie Heiner Friedrich, Munich; Württembergischer Kunstverein, Stuttgart

1979 Galerie Ulysses, Vienna

1980 Nationalgalerie, Berlin. Catalogue with texts by Dieter Honisch, Hermann Kern and the artist. Traveled to Staatliche Kunsthalle Baden-Baden; Städtisches Kunstmuseum, Bonn; Museum Moderner Kunst and Museum des 20. Jahrhunderts, Vienna
Stedelijk van Abbemuseum, Eindhoven, The Netherlands. Catalogue with texts by Rudi Fuchs and the artist. Traveled to Whitechapel Art Gallery, London
Walker Art Center, Minneapolis. Catalogue with text by Lisa Lyons

1982 Suermondt Museum, Aachen
Louisiana Museum of Modern Art, Humlebaek, Denmark
Galerie **m**, Bochum. Catalogue *Hiroshima* with texts by Samuel Beckett, Paul Celan, E. M. Cioran, Heiner Müller, Thomas Pynchon, Jean-Paul Sartre, Peter Weiss and the artist. Traveled to Ulmer Museum, Ulm;

Wilhelm-Hack-Museum, Ludwigshafen; Kunstmuseum Hannover; Malmö Konsthall, Sweden; Museum van Hedendaagse Kunst, Gent; Frankfurter Kunstverein; Kunstmuseum Düsseldorf; Kunsthaus Zürich

1984 Städtisches Museum Mönchengladbach. Catalogue *Mort et Sacrifice* with texts by Johannes Cladders and the artist
Musée National d'Art Moderne, Centre Georges Pompidou, Paris. Catalogue with texts by Anne Albertini, Werner Hofmann, Alfred Pacquement, Armin Zweite and the artist
Stedelijk van Abbemuseum, Eindhoven, The Netherlands. Catalogue with texts by Rudi Fuchs and the artist
Galerie Curtze, Düsseldorf. Catalogue with text by Barbara Catoir

1985 Galerie Maeght Lelong, Zürich. Catalogue with text by Johannes Gachnang
Museum of Modern Art, Oxford, England
Galerie Ulysses, Vienna. Catalogue *Totenmasken* with texts by Werner Hofmann and the artist
Castello di Rivoli, Turin

1986 Ritter Art Gallery, Florida Atlantic University, Boca Raton (coorganizer with Gallery Ulysses, Vienna). Catalogue *Self Portraits* with text by David Courtney. Traveled to University of South Florida Art Galleries, Tampa; Grey Art Gallery and Study Center, New York University; North Carolina Museum of Art, Raleigh; Centre Saidye Bronfman, Montreal
Abbazia di San Gregorio, Venice. Catalogue with text by Rudi Fuchs
Neue Galerie - Sammlung Ludwig, Aaachen. Catalogue with text by Friedhelm Mennekes
Museum Moderner Kunst, Vienna. Catalogue with texts by Hildegund Amanshauser, Andrea Jünger and Otmar Rychlik. Traveled to Kunsthalle Bremen

1987 Magasin, Centre National d'Art Conteporain, Grenoble
Musée des Beaux-Arts, Lausanne. Catalogue with texts by Erika Billeter and the artist. Traveled to Schirn Kunsthalle, Frankfurt
Galerie Ulysses, Vienna. Catalogue *The Cross* with text by the artist
Musées Royaux des Beaux-Arts, Brussels. Catalogue with texts by Otto Breicha, Rudi Fuchs, Werner Hofmann, Armin Zweite and the artist
Museum Overholland, Amsterdam

1988 Museum Haus Lange und Haus Esters, Krefeld. Catalogue with texts by Barbara Catoir, Julian Heynen, Sabine Röder and the artist. Traveled to Neue Galerie, Staatliche und Städtische Kunstsammlungen, Kassel
Hessisches Landesmuseum, Darmstadt
Städtisches Museum, Schloss Morsbroich, Leverkusen. Catalogue with texts by Werner Hofmann, Rolf Wedewer and the artist. Traveled to Städtische Galerie Regensburg; Kunstverein Braunschweig

Selected Group Exhibitions

1951 Institut für Wissenschaft und Kunst, Vienna, *Hundsgruppenausstellung*

1952 Staatsgalerie Stuttgart, *Sammlung Domnick*

1953 Art Institute Chicago, *German Graphic*

1956 Musée d'Art Moderne de la Ville de Paris, *Comparaisons*

1957 Kunstverein, Dusseldorf, *Wiener Secession* Völkerkundemuseum, Hamburg

1959 Dokumenta 2, Kassel

1960 5th International Hallmark Award, New York Galerie Springer, Berlin

1961 Städtische Kunstgalerie, Bochum, West-Germany *Sammlung Schulze-Vellinghausen* Musée d'Art Moderne, Brussels, *Kunst des 20. Jahrhunderts* Arts Council Gallery, London, *österreichische Kunst des 20. Jahrhunderts*

1962 Museum des 20. Jahrhunderts, Vienna, *Kunst von 1900 bis heute*

1963 Stedelijk Museum, Amsterdam, *Schrift und Bild.* Traveled to Kunsthalle, Baden-Baden National Museum of Modern Art, Kyoto, *Contemporary Trends in Painting* Museum des 20. Jahrhunderts, Vienna, *Idole und Dämonen*

1964 Solomon R. Guggenheim Museum, New York, Guggenheim International Award Exhibition Darmstadt, *1. Internationale der Zeichnung* Carnegie International, Pittsburgh

1966 Akademie der Künste, Berlin, *Labyrinthe* Lausanne, *2e Salon International de Galeries Pilotes*

1967 Tokyo, 9th Tokyo Biennial Carnegie International, Pittsburgh

1968 Art Gallery International, Buenos Aires, *1st Graphic Biennal*

1971 Royal Academy, London, *75 Years Vienna Secession* Dublin, *Rosc 71*

1972 Haus der Kunst, Munich, *Weltkulturen und Moderne Kunst* Documenta 5, Kassel

1973 Kunsthalle, Tübingen, *Sammlung Cremer* Städtisches Museum, Leverkusen, *Medium Photographie* Kunstverein Hannover, *Kunst aus Photographie* Steirischer Herbst, Graz, *Körpersprache/Body-language*

1974 Palazzo Reale, Milan, *La Ricerca dell'Identita* Städtische Kunsthalle, Dusseldorf, *Surrealität - Bildrealität*

1975 Museum of Contemporary Art, Chicago, *Bodyworks* Musée d'Ixelles, Brussels, *Je/Nous* Kulturhaus, Graz, *Anfänge des Informel in Österreich 1949-53*

1976 Kunstverein, Frankfurt, *Körpersprache* Centre d'Arts Plastiques Contemporains, Bordeaux *Identite/Identifications*

1977 Dokumenta 6, Kassel Hugh Lane Municipal Gallery of Modern Art and National Museum of Ireland, Dublin, *Rosc 77*

1978 Los Angeles Institute of Contemporary Art, *Museum of Drawers* Gesellschaft der Freunde junger Kunst, Baden-Baden *Positionen der Zeichnung in Österreich*

1979 Art Gallery of New South Wales, Sydney, *European Dialogue: The Third Biennale of Sydney* Hamburger Kunstverein, *Zeichen setzen durch Zeichnen*

1980 The Museum of Modern Art, New York, Printed Art: *A View of Two Decades* Museum Haus Lange, Krefeld, Wendepunkt. *Kunst in Europa um 1960* Venice Biennale, *L'arte negli anni settanta*

1982 Kunstmuseum, Winterthur, Switzerland, *Körperzeichen Österreich*

1983   Solomon R. Guggenheim Museum, New York, *Acquisition Priorities: Aspects of Postwar Painting in Europe*

1984   Castello di Rivoli, Turin, *Ouverture*
Hirshhorn Museum and Sculpture Garden, Smithsonian Institution, Washington, D. C., Content, *A Contemporary Focus 1974-84*

1985   Musée Cantonal des Beaux-Arts, Lausanne and Württembergischer Kunstverein, Stuttgart, *Das Selbstportrait im Zeitalter der Photographie*
Staatsgalerie Moderner Kunst, Munich, *Deutsche Kunst seit 1960 - Sammlung Prinz Franz von Bayern*

1986   Tate Gallery, London, *Forty Years of Modern Art*
Renaissance Society, Chicago
Museum Ludwig, Cologne, *Europa/Amerika*
Los Angeles County Museum of Art, The Spiritual in Art; *Abstract Painting 1890-1985*

Padiglione d'Arte Contemporanea, Milan, *Dal Profondo*

1987   Los Angeles County Museum of Art, *Avantgarde in the Eighties*
The Museum of Modern Art, New York, *Berlinart 1961-87*
Musée National d'Art Moderne, Centre Georges Pompidou, Paris, *Les Dessins Autrichiens*

1988   Art Gallery of New South Wales, Sydney, *The Seventh Biennale of Sydney*
Haags Gemeentemuseum, The Hague, *Collection next the Sea*
Museum Ludwig, Cologne, *Köln sammelt - Zeitgenössische Kunst aus Kölner Privatbesitz*

1989   Museum Ludwig in the Rheinhallen of the Cologne Fair, *Bilderstreit*

Selected Bibliography

Otto Maurer, *Die "Übermalungen" von Arnulf Rainer,* Vienna, 1960. Reprinted with L. Chardon, *Kreuz und Nacht,* Basel, 1960

Werner Hofmann, *Moderne Malerei in Österreich,* Vienna, 1965

Leo Navratil, "Art Brut," *Wort und Wahrheit,* vol. 24, September-October 1969, pp. 452-455

Peter Gorsen, *Das Bild Pygmalions: Kunstsoziologische Essays,* Reinbek, 1969, pp. 169-174

Peter Gorsen, "Diskussion und Kontroverse, Arnulf Rainer," *Wort und Wahrheit,* vol. 25, January-February 1970, pp. 80-83

Peter Weibel and Valie Export, eds., *Wien: Bildkompendium Wiener Aktionismus und Film,* Frankfurt, 1970, pp. 1-8, 241

Otto Breicha, *Arnulf Rainer, Überdeckungen, Oeuvrekatalog der Druckgraphik 1950-71,* Vienna, 1971

Reinhard Priessnitz, "Untergrund, Hintergrund, Aktionismus," *Ver Sacrum: Neue Hefte für Kunst und Literatur* (Vienna), 1971

Hilde Schmölzer, *Das böse Wien: Gespräche mit österreichischen Künstlern,* Munich, 1973, pp. 160-168

Barbara Catoir, "Interview mit Arnulf Rainer," *Das Kunstwerk,* January 1975

Jean-Jacques Lévèque, "Le Body-Art ou le corps agressé," *Les Nouvelles Littéraires,* January 13-19, 1975

Gordon Brown, "Arnulf Rainer, Dieter Rot," *Arts Magazine,* September 1975

Eduard Beaucamp, "Die schwarzen Pantomimen eines Malers," *Frankfurter Allgemeine Zeitung,* November 24, 1975

Max Kozloff, "Pygmalion Reversed," *Artforum,* November 1975, p. 33

Werner Lippert, "Das Selbstportrait als Bildtypus," *Kunstforum International,* vol. 14, 1975, pp. 99-124

Achille Bonito-Oliva, *Europe-America: The Different Avant-Gardes,* Milan, 1976

Jacques Clayssen, "Entretien avec Arnulf Rainer," in *Identité-Identification,* exh. cat., Centre d'Arts Plastiques Contemporains, Bordeaux, 1976

Petr Tausk, *Die Geschichte der Fotografie im 20. Jahrhundert,* Cologne, 1977, pp. 169f

Arnulf Rainer, "Hundert bildnerische Serien," *Kunstforum International,* vol. 26, no. 2, 1978

Georg Schwarzbauer, "Arnulf Rainer," *Kunstforum International,* vol. 26, no. 2, 1978, pp. 222-231

Hanne Weskott, "Performances 1979," *Kunstforum International,* no. 32, 1979, pp. 172-181

Otto Breicha, ed., *Arnulf Rainer, Hirndrang, Selbstkommentare und andere Texte zu Werk und Person mit 118 Bildbeigaben,* Salzburg, 1980

Barbara Catoir, "Der Wahn, das Häßliche, die Destruktion, die Komik und der Tod," in *A. R. Körpersprache,* Munich, 1980, pp. 182-189

Arnulf Rainer and Brigitte Schwaiger, *Malstunde,* Vienna and Hamburg, 1980

Werner Hofmann, "übermalt, überzeichnet, zerschürft oder zerkratzt," in *Max Beckmann-Preis,* exh. cat., Frankfurt, 1981

Michelangelo Castello, "Morte e trasfigurazione: Arnulf Rainer," *Tema Celeste,* June 1985

Johannes Gachnang, "Fragespiel mit Arnulf Rainer," in *Reisebilder - Berichte zur zeitgenössischen Kunst,* Vienna, 1985

Friedhelm Mennekes, "Kunst aus Distanzierung," in *Arnulf Rainer: Umkreisen und Durchdringen,* Stuttgart, 1986

Donald Kuspit, "Arnulf Rainer: Self-Exposures," *Art in America,* April 1987

Guy Scarpetta, "Pour Arnulf Rainer," *Art Press,* January 1989, p. 19

Guy Scarpetta, "Arnulf Rainer: Je ne suis pas un profanateur," *Art Press,* January 1989, pp. 20-24

Barbara Catoir, *Übermalte Bücher,* Munich, 1989

Otmar Rychlik, ed., *Rainerianer, Aufsätze zum Werk von Arnulf Rainer,* Wien, 1989

Photographic Credits

Exhibition 89/2
900 copies of this catalogue have been published in April 1989 by ARGE
Gabriele Wimmer & John Sailer, Vienna, for the Trustees of the Solomon R. Guggenheim Foundation
on the occasion of the exhibition *Arnulf Rainer*.